Sydney Barrington Elliot

Aedoeology

A Treatise on Generative Life

Sydney Barrington Elliot

Aedoeology
A Treatise on Generative Life

ISBN/EAN: 9783337373030

Printed in Europe, USA, Canada, Australia, Japan

Cover: Foto ©Lupo / pixelio.de

More available books at **www.hansebooks.com**

ÆDŒOLOGY

A Treatise on Generative Life.

Including Pre-Natal Influence, Limitation of Offspring,
and Hygiene of the Generative System.

A BOOK FOR EVERY MAN AND WOMAN

By Sydney Barrington Elliot, M. D.

"IT IS THE RIGHT OF EVERY CHILD TO BE WELL BORN."

BOSTON:
ARENA PUBLISHING Co.,
COPLEY SQUARE.
1893.

To ALL WHO WISH TO BRING INTO THE WORLD HEALTHY

CHILDREN, PHYSICALLY AND MENTALLY, AND LIVE

TOGETHER PURE, NATURAL LIVES,

THIS BOOK IS DEDICATED.

PREFACE.

WHEN the author first became interested in this subject, he was surprised at the almost universal ignorance and prejudice concerning it. This fact, and the widespread interest which was taken in an article read at one of our medical meetings and published in several medical journals, convinced him that a scientific study of the whole ground, with the practical deductions therefrom, would be of much value to both lay and professional reader. To do this and make it thorough and convincing, it was found necessary to review a great deal of medical literature in different languages ; from which were gathered many extracts from noted authorities, and many cases of prenatal influence, or maternal impressions, as they are there called.

Of these extracts which have been gathered, a few have been selected and given in different parts of the book ; of the cases gathered, some five

hundred have been given either in detail or referred to, fearing to burden the book by giving
more.

While pre-natal influence has been widely written upon in medical literature, as will be seen
from this part of the book, such writing has been
done in a fragmentary manner. No writer has
ever collated sufficient proof of this influence to be
convincing, and to use such to show how it may be
applied for the benefit of the race. Besides those
whose writings on this subject have been recorded
in medical literature, a few have dealt with it to a
certain extent in a popular form, but the subject
has never been investigated on a scientific basis
and put in such a way that any practical results
could ensue.

Neither time nor pains has been spared in insur-
ing the reliability of quotations and cases. That
much benefit should result from this investigation,
there is little doubt. Let the reader weigh carefully the facts and arguments given, and we have
no fear for the results.

It is the author's intention to supply physicians
with a book covering this ground, which they
can place with confidence in the hands of their patients, thus saving themselves much time which

the necessary explanation of this subject would require.

I wish especially to express my obligations, for many kind suggestions and much assistance, to Dr. George F. Laidlaw, of New York.

Louisville, Ky.

CONTENTS.

PART III.

HYGIENE AND PHYSIOLOGY OF GENERATIVE LIFE.

INTRODUCTION.

―――――

" Cruel and cold is the judgment of man,
   Cruel as winter, and cold as the snow ;
But by and by will the deed and the plan
   Be judged by the motive that lieth below."
                                    ――BATES.

THE process by which man is born into this world, and the circumstances which go to make him what he is, whether it be a theologian or a scapegrace, a mathematician or a fool, concerns all.

It is a subject of universal interest and of vital importance, whether it be considered from a physical, moral, social or medical standpoint. It lies at the foundation of all human improvement and enduring progress.

The function of reproduction, as examined into by the most scientific physiologists and moralists, is considered to be the most influential function of the human economy ; yet in spite of this, it is a subject which is ignored in text-books on physiology, it is not taught in medical colleges and physicians, as a rule, say very little about it.

It is a sad reflection upon our civilization that people should be left to live, propagate and bring up children in entire darkness of this most important of all subjects ; while every trade, profession and occupation, and all other branches of physiology are taught and have light thrown upon them for the benefit of all.

The subject is an extremely difficult one with which to deal, for it is hedged around by the prejudice which is born of ignorance, and few dare to surmount the barrier. Many allow a sort of mock-modesty to step in and keep them from investigating this most important of all subjects. Could these, however, be persuaded to examine the subject with unbiassed minds, and to lay aside prejudice—for as that illustrious writer, Lord Lytton, has well said, '' Vice has no friend like the prejudice which claims to be virtue''--they could not help from deriving much benefit.

In ancient times the physical side of man dominated the intellectual ; in more modern times the intellectual ruled the physical ; and now the time has come for the moral faculties to govern the intellectual and all others.

Expectant parents should know how to have well-born children or none at all; and, furthermore, these and all others, if they wish to live healthy, natural lives, must have at least some knowledge of the generative system.

This subject divides itself naturally into three parts. Part First deals with pre-natal influence and the requisites for having a well-born child. .

Part Second tells those who, from whatever cause, cannot have well-born children how conception may be avoided.

Part Third deals with hygiene of the reproductive system, following the being through all the phases of generative life.

.

PART I.

PRE=NATAL INFLUENCE.

———

CHAPTER I.

Nature and Importance of Pre-natal Influence.

" But truths on which depends our main concern,
    That 'tis our shame and misery not to learn,
    Shine by the side of every path we tread
    With such a lustre, he that runs may read."
                                        —COWPER.

By the term **Pre-natal (or Ante-natal) Influence** we mean all influences, physical, mental, or moral, which, acting through the parents, affect an un-born child. These forces are not active during actual pregnancy only, for the condition of both father and mother some little time before and at conception helps to determine the form and char-acter of the offspring.

Heredity is that law by which permanent and

settled qualities of the parents or of the more re-
mote ancestors reappear in the child ; while pre-
natal influence signifies the effect produced upon
the future being by temporary conditions of the
parents in the above periods, as by temporary
mental states (anger, fear, happiness), or by temporary physical conditions (activity, health, exhaustion of a part or of the entire body).

Who has not observed that children of the same
parents, born within a few years of each other,
are often totally unlike in disposition, in strength,
and in ability ? They may be not only unlike
each other, but unlike the parents themselves.
The law of heredity would require the constitution of the child to be made up of the personal
characteristics of each parent, altered, perhaps,
by many streams of influence coming from the
ancestors on each side.   But we find virtuous and
well-meaning parents, with long lines of repu-
table ancestry, bringing forth vicious and obsti-
nate children ; and, on the other hand, the igno
rant and vulgar sometimes producing children
that are remarkable for special ability or refinement.   It must be acknowledged that some forces
are at work other than heredity as the term is
generally understood.

That these forces which modify or distort hereditary tendencies are *pre-natal*, as we have defined
that term above, it is our object to prove. Opinions expressed by the ablest and most acute observers among the medical profession, some of
which we quote, lift this question out of the
realm of old women's notions and place it upon a
footing where it demands investigation by all
who presume to become parents. Cases will be
given in which the state of the mother, her emotions, her experiences, and her actions have had
an undoubted effect upon the child she has
borne ; this effect being favorable or unfavorable
according to the kind of influence. It will be
proved that decided effects from pre-natal influences can occur, and we will urge upon the reader
the importance of making those influences favorable, or at least of guarding against those that
are harmful.

As to the manner in which this process is carried on, we must confess that there is some ob-
scurity. This, however, does not in any way
modify the fact that such a process does take
place. There seems to be a subtle sympathy
between mother and child, organ for organ, part
for part. The child's body is growing rapidly in

all directions, building material is plentiful, and
the energies that can utilize it seem tireless. If
any portion of the mother's body, whether it be
an intellectual faculty or the stomach, is either
continuously or *intensely* active, the same portion
in the child seems to be stimulated to increased
growth ; and increased growth means increased
power. It does not seem necessary that the
mother should possess either the physical or mental power that she can produce in the child ; for
in the case of Zerah Colburn (page 74) the mother
had little arithmetical ability, while the son's
powers were remarkable. It is merely necessary
to have intense or continuous *effort* on the mother's part in order to stimulate the special growth
in the child.

The manner in which the influence is produced
on the father's side is still more obscure. The
seed seems stamped with the imprint not only of
his permanent characteristics (heredity), but also
of his temporary conditions of mind and body
(pre-natal influence), and these have their place
in determining the character of the offspring.

In confirmation of the foregoing statements, we
submit extracts from the writings of men eminent
in the science of physiology, whose opinions on

this subject are not easily accessible to the general public. These authors, with hardly an exception, like most others who have given any attention to this matter, have done so strictly from a scientific point of view, and have never given the results of their investigations in a popular form so that any practical results could ensue for the " betterment of mankind."

OPINIONS OF EMINENT AUTHORITIES.

" The wisdom of the wise, and the experience of ages, may be preserved by quotation."—DISRAELI.

The late Fordyce Barker, M.D., LL.D., one of the most eminent physicians in America, read an excellent paper, entitled " The Influence of Maternal Impressions on the Fœtus," before the American Gynæcological Society (in the year 1886), in which he says : " *Maternal impressions may affect the development, form and character of the fœtus.*" In speaking of the blood being the agent through which maternal impressions are conveyed, he says : " Food, medicines, poisons and diseases are conveyed to the fœtus *in utero.* Children are born with measles, scarlet-fever, small-pox and other communicable diseases. Congenital chorea, hysteria and epilepsy have been observed. Mothers who have suffered a severe fright when advanced in pregnancy have given birth to choreic children." He cites many good cases, some of which will be referred to again.

Carpenter wrote as follows : " That the mental state of the mother can produce important alterations in her own blood seems demonstrated by the considerations previously advanced in regard to its effect upon the processes of nutrition and secretion, and that such alterations are sufficient to determine important modifications in the developmental processes of the embryo, to which her blood furnishes the material, can scarcely admit of a question, when we recollect what an influence the presence or absence of particular substances has in modifying the growth of parts in the adult."

Bichat says : " It is by the modifications which the mother's blood receives from vivid emotions that we must explain their influence upon nutrition, the growth, and even the life of the foetus, to which the blood is supplied through the placenta."[1]

---

[1] L. i., p. 43.

Dalton says, in speaking of pre-natal influence :
" We know very well how easily nervous impressions will disturb the circulation in the brain, the
face, the lungs, etc., and the interior circulation is
quite as readily influenced by similar causes, as
physicians see every day in cases of amenorrhœa,
menorrhagia, etc. If a nervous shock may excite
premature contraction in the muscular fibres of the
pregnant uterus, and produce abortion, as not infre-
quently happens, it is certainly capable of disturbing the course of the circulation through the same
organ. But the fœtal circulation is dependent to
a great extent on the maternal, since the two sets
of vessels are so closely entwined in the placenta ;
and since the fœtal blood has here much the same
relation to the maternal that the blood in the pul-
monary capillaries has to the air in the air vessels,
it will be liable to derangement from similar
causes. If the circulation of air through the pul-
monary tubes and vessels be suspended, that of
the blood through the capillaries comes to an end
also. In the same way, whatever disturbs or arrests the circulation through the vessels of the
maternal uterus must necessarily be liable to interfere with that in the fœtal capillaries forming
part of the placenta ; and lastly, as the nutrition

of the fœtus is provided for wholly by the placental circulation, it will of course suffer immediately
from any such disturbance of the placental circulation.   The effects may be manifested either in
the general atrophy and death of the fœtus, or, if
the disturbing cause be slight, in the atrophy or
imperfect development of particular parts ; just
as, in the adult, a morbid cause operating through
the entire system may be first or even exclusively
manifested in some particular organ which is
more sensitive to its influence than other parts."

Dr. Brittan, who has given much study to the
occult problems of human life, in writing of the
" Relations of Mind to Offspring," gives the following as to the law or process of embryonic
moulding : " The singular effects produced on
the unborn child by the sudden mental emotions
of the mother are remarkable examples of a kind
of electrotyping on the sensitive surfaces of living forms.   It is doubtless true that the mind's
action in such cases may increase or diminish the
molecular deposits in the several portions of the
system.   The precise place which each separate
particle assumes in the new organic structure may
be determined by the influence of thought or feeling.   If, for example, there exists in the mother

any unusual tendency of the vital forces to the brain at the critical period, there will be a similar cerebral development and activity in the offspring."

Plato,[1] after discussing how easily impressions are stamped upon infants, says : " Nay, more, I would say that a woman during her time of pregnancy should of all women be most carefully tended, and kept from violent and excessive pleasures and pains ; and at that time she should cultivate gentleness, benevolence and kindness."

A. Combe[2] says, in reference to pre-natal influence : " If a sudden and powerful emotion of her own mind exerts such an influence upon her stomach as to excite vomiting, and upon her heart as almost to arrest its motion and induce fainting, can we believe that it will have no effect upon her womb and the fragile being contained within it ? Facts and reason, then, alike demonstrate the reality of the influence, and much practical advantage would result to both parent and child were the conditions and extent of its operations better understood."

---

[1] Seventh Book of Laws.
[2] On the Management of Infancy.

One writer even says : '' The fundamental principles of genius in reproduction are that through
the rightly directed influence of the wills of the
mother and father, preceding and during ante-
natal life, the child's form of body, character of
mind and purity of soul are formed and estab-
lished ; that in its plastic state during ante-natal
life, like clay in the hands of the potter, it can be
moulded into absolutely any form of body and
soul the parents may knowingly desire.''

Spurzheim, in his '' Education,'' says : '' The
innate constitution, which depends upon both
parents and the state of the mother during pregnancy, are the basis of all future development.''

Dr. Stockham, in that well-known book '' Tokology,'' says, when speaking of the deplorable
results following the present mode of living and
begetting children : '' Future generations demand
that such results be averted by pre-natal influences.''

MM. Grimaud de Caux and **Martin St. Ange**[1]
say on this subject : '' Pregnancy is a function of
the woman, as are digestion and the acts of secretion of various kinds, and if these latter are affect-

---

[1] '' Histoire de la Génération de l'Homme, etc.,'' Paris, 1849, p. 252.

ed by moral impressions, why should not the former be also similarly acted upon? If the composition of the blood be altered, is it possible that the fœtus which is being developed in the mother's womb by this fluid should not undergo changes?''

Devay[1] says: '' Both reason and experience establish the fact that mental impressions of the mother may influence the fœtus so as to give rise to an aberration of which *the form will correspond to the emotion acting upon the mother.*''

Selden H. Talcott[2] says: '' Those who are born to become insane do not necessarily spring from insane parents, or from an ancestry having any apparent taint of lunacy in their blood, but they do receive from their progenitors certain impressions upon their mental and moral, as well as their physical beings, which impressions, like an iron mould, fix and shape their subsequent destinies. Hysteria in the mother may develop the insane diathesis in the child, while drunkenness in the father may impel epilepsy, or mania, or dementia in the son. Ungoverned passions in the parents

---

[1] '' Traité spéciale d'Hygiène des Familles,'' Paris, 1858, p. 329.
[2] In an article entitled '' The Insane Diathesis.''

may unloose the furies of unrestrained madness in the minds of their children. Even untempered religious enthusiasm may beget a fanaticism that cannot be restrained within the limits of reason.

"Unpleasant influences brought to bear upon the helpless mother during the delicate period of pregnancy, or a free exercise of unholy passions in her heart while thus living a duplex life, are so marked by the production of a vast variety of mental peculiarities that historical, scientific and medical works are replete with the unhappy records. The influence of a predominant passion may be transmitted from the parent to the child, just as surely as facial contours or expressions. It has been truly said that 'the faculties which predominate in power and activity in the parents, when the organic existence of the child commences, determine its future mental disposition.'"

Rokitansky[1] says: "The question whether mental emotions do influence the development of the embryo (unborn child) must be answered in the affirmative."

Dr. Oliver Wendell Holmes makes pre-natal in-

---

[1] Path. Anat., vol. i., p. 11.

fluence the groundwork for his remarkable novel, "Elsie Venner."

Paulus Ægineta[1] and others give some interesting quotations from ancient authors, who believed in pre-natal influence. **Galen** (*ad Pisonum*), **Soranus, Hesiod, Heliodorus** and **Hippocrates** are especially quoted.

Ambroise Paré,[2] in Book XXV., entitled " Of Monsters and Prodigies," describes and figures many instances ; and in chapter vii. he very distinctly avows his belief in pre-natal influence.

Montgomery[3] says : " Pregnant women should not be exposed to causes likely to distress or otherwise strongly impress their minds."

Dr. Lewis A. Sayre[4] says : " We all admit that it is by the nerves we receive impressions ; that it is through them that the will is conveyed to the different parts of the system ; that the vessels are the executors of the will ; and that secretion,

[1] Sydenham Society Transl., 1844, Commentary on Book I.

[2] London, 1634.

[3] "Signs and Symptoms of Pregnancy," Philadelphia, 1857, p. 29.

[4] " Facts and Arguments on the Transmission of Intellectual and Moral Qualities from Parents to Offspring," New York, T. Winchester, publisher, 2d ed.

absorption, the different growths, developments, etc., are the result of this work carried on or performed by the vessels and controlled by the nerves ; or, in other words, the brain and nervous mass superintends or orders, the vessels obey these orders, and the different growths, etc., are the result of the work.

" If, then, the nervous system or controlling power be disturbed, the orders are given wrong ; the vessels obeying these wrong orders, and acting in compliance with them, an unnatural or deformed product is the necessary result.

" We all admit, again, that the child has not an independent existence until extra-uterine life ; neither has it an independent will ; but it also is dependent upon the mother, is under her control, and must, of course, act in accordance with hers.

" If, then, the will, thought, impressions, mind, or controlling power, so to speak, exist entirely in the brain and nervous masses, when endowed with life (as without them we can receive no impressions), and if the vessels act entirely under the control of these nerves, and the different growths, developments, etc., are the result of the action of these vessels, and if the will of the child is dependent entirely upon that of the mother, it follows, as a matter of course, the developments of the child being the result of the action of its vessels, which vessels are controlled by its nervous system, and it again entirely dependent on the . mother, that these various developments must be in accordance with the various impressions made upon her mind.

" Again, it is generally admitted concerning any system, whether nervous, vascular or muscular, that it is capable of performing function in an exalted or diminished degree according to its developments as regards strength and activity.

" If, then, we admit that by the exercise of organs we increase their power of performing function—as is proved by comparing the arm of the blacksmith with that of the writing-master— and also that the brain is the seat of the intellect or mind—as proved by acephalous children, who, having no brain, are deficient in its Godlike attributes—and if the mental organs can be increased in power as well as the physical, and if the child's organs are developed in harmony with the mother's, with what vast importance do we find this interesting question surrounded, and what strong appeals from future generations are made upon the fondly expecting-to-be mother to exercise both her physical and mental powers to their greatest degree, in order that she may be the happy bearer of an offspring gifted in these essentials for future usefulness in their highest degree of development, both as regards strength and activity."

The **Spartans** surrounded their wives, while pregnant, with beautiful pictures, images, and statues, such as those of Castor and Pollux, who represented strength and beauty, and enforced that custom by the requirements of law (the law of Lycurgus). It is not surprising, then, that they were physically such a fine race of people.

To the authorities already given, as well as those who have given cases as recorded in subsequent chapters, I add the names of the following, all of whom express their belief positively in prenatal influence : **Elliotson,**[1] **Flint,**[2] **Foster, Gillman, Hammond,**[3] **Sir Everard Home, Malpighi,**[4] **Richardson, Roth, Isidore Geoffroy Saint-Hilaire,**[5]

---

[1] Elliotson's " Physiology."

[2] Flint's " Physiology."

[3] " Treatise on Insanity," p. 2.

[4] In his " De Formatione Pulli in Ovo."

[5] " Hist. gén. et partie des anomalies, de l'organisation chez l'homme et les animaux," Bruxelles, 1837, tome iii., p. 377.

Seguin, Spitzka, Allen Thompson,[1] Tuke,[2] and others *ad lib.*

Biblical Evidence.—As far back as the days of Jacob this law was understood and practised, for in the Book of Genesis we are told that "Jacob took him rods of green poplar, and of the hazel and chestnut-tree, and pilled white streaks in them, and made the white appear which was in the rods. And he set the rods which he had pilled before the flocks in the gutters in the watering-troughs when the flocks came to drink, that they should conceive when they came to drink. And the flocks conceived before the rods, and brought forth cattle, ring-streaked, speckled, and spotted. . . . And it came to pass, whensoever the stronger cattle did conceive, that Jacob laid the rods before the eyes of the cattle in the gutters, that they might conceive among the rods. But when the cattle were feeble, he put them not in ; so the feebler were Laban's, and the stronger, Jacob's."

———

Having in this chapter defined pre-natal influence, and given the opinions of many eminent

---

[1] "Cyclopedia of Anatomy and Physiology," vol. ii., p. 474.
[2] "Influence of the Mind upon the Body."

physiologists, we are now prepared to give examples of actual cases. These will be divided into
two classes, our next chapter being devoted to cases
in which the influence has been unfavorable ; while
most of those related in the third chapter have
resulted favorably, illustrating how pre-natal influence may be taken advantage of to better the
offspring.

CHAPTER II.

Cases.

" When fiction rises pleasing to the eye,
    Men will believe because they love the lie ;
But truth herself, if clouded with a frown,
    Must have some solemn proof to pass her down."
                     —CHURCHILL.

THIS chapter was compiled especially for physicians into whose hands this book may come. The medical mind is conservative ; it requires strong and repeated evidence before it will assent to new and unaccustomed doctrines. Examples sufficient to prove pre-natal influence exist in medical literature, but they have never been collated in sufficient numbers to convince the great body of the profession.

Although a single well-observed and carefully tested fact is sufficient to upset a dozen theories, many cases from undoubted sources will be given. The cases will be divided into classes, according to the nature of the impression on the mother and the result on the fœtus.

On account of the space they would require,

we are unable to give as many cases in each class
as we would like, but many more similar to those
of every class, even those affecting the lower
animals, will be found in the list, pp. 53–64.   Owing
to the large number of cases recorded, it is essential that they should be given as briefly as possible,
but the main points in each case have been carefully preserved.

There are many such cases in medical literature, but, strange to say, they are recorded as
freaks of nature ; they have never been given as
evidence to show the wonderful, almost unlimited
extent of this influence, and how it may be taken
advantage of to better the race.   The truth of
these cases is undoubted ; and this fact of being
true, with the great principle they establish, is
sufficient explanation for their admission to the
book.

Cases in which the Offspring has been Af-
fected Mentally, or Mentally and Physi-
cally, by Mental Emotions of the Mother.

Many such cases are on record, and are given
by such authorities as **Putzel, Mayo, Richter,
Spamer, Hammond, Seguin,** etc.

Spamer gives a case where the child was an idiot as a result of the mother's nervous and depressed condition during pregnancy, owing to the death of a child.

Dr. Bailey[1] gives a case where a child was affected with convulsions from birth as a result of the mother having nursed another child through an attack of cerebro-spinal meningitis.

Dr. Seguin[2] reports the following case, which came under his own observation and care : A girl, who at the time he knew her was twelve or thirteen years old, was a congenital idiot ; the other members of the family, which was a large one, were above the average in point of intelligence. The mother was pregnant with this idiotic child during the civil war of Paris, and was harassed with anxiety for the safety of her husband.

The result of mental emotions of the mother upon the fœtus, as a result of war and like disasters, has long been noted, as in **the Siege of Landau,**—recorded by **Baron Percy,** and quoted by Carpenter, Pinel, and others. At the siege of Landau, in France, in 1793, there was

---

[1] *Med. and Surg. Reporter* of May 31st, 1873.

[2] *Phila. Med. Times,* 1867, vol. ii., pp. 121-123.

such violent cannonading that the women were kept in a constant state of alarm. In addition, the arsenal blew up with a terrific explosion, which few could hear with unshaken nerves. The result was, out of 92 children born in that district within a few months, 16 died at birth, 33 languished for eight or ten months and died, 8 became idiots, and died before they were five years old, and 2 came into the world with numerous fractures of the limbs. The history of the others was not followed up, but it is doubtful if they escaped without injury, though it may have been of a less serious nature.

Results of French Revolution.—Esquirol, a famous French writer, mentions that many children, born when the horrors of the French Revolution were at the highest, turned out to be weak, nervous and irritable, and liable to insanity.

Results of Siege of Antwerp.—It has also been noted that of the children born at the siege of Antwerp, a large proportion was deformed, and many were still-born.

Results of Financial Crises in Berlin.—It has been recorded [1] that the financial crises in Berlin

---

[1] *Neurologische Centralblatt*, p. 499.

were followed by an increased number of idiots born.

The case of one of the kings of England is a notable one, and is known to all history.

James I. of England.—The murder of David Rizzio was perpetrated by armed nobles, with vio-lence and terror, in the presence of Mary, Queen of Scotland, shortly before the birth of her son, James I. of England.'' The liability of this mon-arch to emotions of fear is recorded as a promi-nent characteristic of his mind, and so great was his terror of a sword—the weapon with which Rizzio was killed—that he would shudder at the sight of it. Sir Digby relates that when King James conferred the knighthood upon him, which is done by laying a naked sword upon the shoul-der of the new knight, he could not look at the sword, but turned his head away, so that he came very near putting the point into the knight's eye.

Sir Kinelm was saved from a similar catas-trophe by the Duke of Buckingham, who in the nick of time guided the sword aright.[1]

---

[1] A discourse made in solemn assembly of nobles and learned men at Montpellier, France, and rendered out of French into English by R. White, London, 1658,

Queen Mary was not deficient in courage, and the Stuarts, both before and after James I., were distinguished for this quality, so that his disposition was an exception to the family character, and due to pre-natal influence.

Dr. Seguin[1] states a case very similar to that of James I. : An officer of the old Napoleon, known for his bravery in the field, would become pale and faint at the sight of a naked parlor sword. It was well known that before he was born his father had all but killed his mother with such an arm, in a fit of jealousy.

Sir Arthur Mitchell, Commissioner in Lunacy for Scotland, has made some valuable investigations as to pre-natal influence.[2] From 443 cases of idiocy or imbecility, examined with special reference to the effect of " strong mental emotion affecting pregnant women as a cause of idiocy in the offspring," he has, in his article read at this society, selected cases which did not in the history of the children present any other circumstances which " had a preferential claim to be considered the cause of the imperfection." Of the

---

[1] *Phila. Med. Times,* 1876–77, vol. li., pp. 121–123.

[2] Trans. Obst. Soc., London, vol. xxvi., p. 127.

cases he has selected, we give the two following :

" A woman, while pregnant, witnessed from the shore the drowning of her husband, a fisherman, during a storm. She was in a deplorable state of terror while watching his danger, and fainted when the catastrophe came. Long afterward she remained in feeble health. Her child, when born, was small and weakly, and turned out an idiot."

The second case is that of a woman who, while pregnant, lost three of her children in one week of epidemic fever. Her grief and agitation at the time were excessive, overwhelming ; and she continued in a state of deep depression, never quitting her bedroom till she was delivered, several months after the bereavement, being then in a wretched state of bodily health. Her child was an idiot.

Cases in which the Offspring has been Affected Physically, due to Physical Impressions on the Mother.

Dr. Hart[1] reports a case where the mother,

---

[1] *Am. Jour. of Med. Sci.*, January, 1881.

when she was eight and a half months pregnant, was burned extensively on the body and limbs. Thirty-six hours afterward she was delivered of a still-born child with large, fresh-looking blebs, corresponding in site exactly to the burns of the mother.

Dr. Niker[1] reports the following case : A woman, near the end of her pregnancy, received burns upon her hand, and when the child was born it had fresh-looking blebs upon its hand, corresponding in position to the mother's burns.

Dr. T. A. Martyn[2] cites another such case. A woman was severely burned about the legs. She miscarried in six hours. The corresponding parts of the fœtus were blistered, and had the same appearance of those of the mother.

Dr. S. O. Stockslager reports the following case :[3] A woman (a multipara) whom he attended in confinement said she was afraid her baby would be marked, as two months before she had burned her wrists. Dr. S. ridiculed the idea,

---

[1] *Obst. Jour. Gr. Brit.*, June 15th, 1880.

[2] *Am. Jour. of Med. Sci.*

[3] *Chicago Med. Jour. and Exam.* of May 23d, 1881, vol. xliii., p. 313.

saying " there was no likelihood of it, and to quiet herself and not cross the bridge till she came to it. But lo ! when the child was born, about two hours afterward, there was the exact counterpart of the mother's burns."

Other cases where the mother has suffered from a burn during pregnancy, and which has resulted in the child's being similarly affected in the same place, will be found in the list, p. 53.

Dr. Fordyce Barker cites the following case,[1] which we quote in full : " Mrs. A——, who had been married but a few weeks, was at the theatre with her husband and other friends. Something, she knew not what, vexed him, and he placed the point of his elbow on her hand, which was resting on the arm of her seat, and held it so firmly that she could not draw it away. Not wishing to make a scene in the theatre, she bore it silently until she fainted. The fingers were much swollen and very painful for several days. She never lived with her husband afterward, and subsequently obtained a divorce on the ground of cruelty. Thirty-five weeks and three days after

---

[1] Article on " Maternal Impressions," read before the Am. Gyn-æcological Society, 1886.

the theatre incident, I attended her, when she gave birth to a son. On the left hand, the first and second phalanges (bones) of all the fingers and the thumb were absent, looking as if they had been amputated. She has lived abroad most of the time since the divorce. I saw her in London, in August last, for the first time in several years, and examined the hand of the lad, now fifteen years old, and unusually bright and clever. In reply to a question from me, which she says I had repeatedly asked in the infancy of her child, she assured me that never once during her pregnancy had the thought occurred to her that her child would be born with this deficiency.''

Roth[1] cites a case where the child was born with a cystic tumor on its neck as a result of the mother being stabbed in the neck when she was about three months pregnant.

Dr. A. M. Brown[2] gives the case of a woman who had her ears pierced, and was much disturbed afterward for fear of its effect on the child. When the child was born it had holes in the lobules of its ears.

---

[1] Virchow's Archiv., Band xci.

[2] *Brit. Med. Jour.*, February 20th, 1886.

Dr. **Doane**[1] reports the case of a pregnant woman who had one of her ears torn through by the forcible dragging away of one of her earrings. Her child was born with a fissure in the ear corresponding to the laceration in the mother.

Dr. Wilson reports the following case :[2] The child of Mrs. T—— was born with a mark on its back and also one on the centre of its forehead. The mother had during the fourth month of her pregnancy received a blow on the lumbar region, and a month later was struck on her forehead by something falling.

Cases in which the Child has been Affected Physically, due to the Mother's Mental Impressions.

The following case is given by **Fordyce Barker**,[3] which we quote in full :

" A lady was married at the age of twenty, when her father made her a present of a house. She was absent on her wedding trip for two weeks, and then went to the Gramercy Park

---

[1] *Am. Jour. Med. Sci.*, vol. xxv., p. 358.

[2] *Obst. Jour., Gr. Brit. and Ire.*, vol. viii., p. 333.

[3] Tr. Gynæcological Society, 1886.

Hotel to stay while her house was being repainted
and decorated, and such furniture as she wished
was selected and purchased. She had not men-
struated since her marriage. On her first day at
this hotel she went to the *table d'hôte*, and found
herself seated opposite a gentleman with three
daughters, who all had hare-lips. (This family
was well known.) The first glance at them made
her so faint that she at once left the table, and
always after took her meals in her private rooms
until she moved to her own house. She never
mentioned her reasons for this even to her husband, nor had she any suspicion that she was
pregnant. I attended her in her confinement,
which was a very laborious one, and she was delivered by the forceps, profoundly under the influence of chloroform. I saw at once that the
child had a double hare-lip, and sent for Dr. Car-
nochan, who had finished the operation before
she awoke from the chloroform sleep. On becoming conscious, she demanded to see her child,
saying that she was certain that it had a hare-lip.
I refused to allow her to see the child until the
next morning, and gave her a full opiate. The
operation was remarkably successful, the mother
did well, and the child, now nearly thirty, would

not attract attention by the appearance of his lip, but only by an indistinct articulation of a few words.'' Dr. Barker goes on to say :

" **Dr. Hunter McGuire,** of Richmond, Va., related to me the following case, of which he was cognizant : A slave, in order to avoid being sold to another family, cut off one of his great toes with an axe, in the presence of his pregnant mistress. When her child was born, one foot was without a toe, and the stump greatly resembled that of the negro. Dr. McGuire was not able to inform me as to the period of pregnancy when the self-amputation of the negro occurred, but he added that he could not learn that the lady had ever anticipated the mutilation of her child.''

Malebranche quotes **Gaharliep**[1] as declaring that his own son was born with his right hand distorted and dislocated in consequence of his mother having seen from her carriage, eight days before her delivery, a man with his hand in these conditions.

Dr. Kerr reports the following case :[2] A pregnant woman, whose little daughter fell against a

---

[1] Recherche de la verité.
[2] *Amer. Jour. Med. Sci.,* vol. xxiv., p. 285.

hot cooking-stove and was badly burned on the face, hands and arms, was greatly shocked and frightened. She frequently referred to the accident. Three months afterward her child was born marked with blisters on the lips, in the mouth, on the right ear, right elbow, both hands, each knee, and both ankles, resembling those caused by the burns.

Dr. Hammond gives the following case :[1] A lady at the third month of her pregnancy was horrified at the appearance of her husband with a severe wound of the face. She was afraid her child would be marked, and it was ; for when born it was seen to have a mark on the face corresponding in situation and extent with that which had been upon the father's face.

Dr. Bayard[2] tells of a woman who, when *enceinte*, witnessed a fire in the direction of her father's home, and was much alarmed ; as the event proved, not without reason. As the place was many miles distant, a long time passed without any definite tidings. This uncertainty acted powerfully upon her imagination, and she con-

---

[1] *Psych. Jour.*, vol. ii., 1868.
[2] *Annales Médico-Psychologique*, 1851, p. 478.

stantly saw a flame before her eyes. Three months afterward she gave birth to a child which had on the forehead a red, pointed and undulated mark, like a flame ; this mark was not effaced until she was seven years of age. **Baer,** in reporting this circumstance, says that he does so because he has the best means of knowing all the details, seeing that the lady was his own sister, and that he had heard her complain before her accouchement of having a flame continually before her eyes.

Professor L. Neugebauer[1] gives two or three cases, at the conclusion of one of which he says : " I, on my part, do not doubt the influence of maternal impressions upon the fœtus ; my own son serves me as a proof of it. I once hurt my leg on the inside by a thorn while bathing in a river. On my return home, at the moment when I was dressing the wound, my wife, who was then pregnant, entered, and was frightened by it. The boy born in due course has, in the same place where I have the scar resulting from the wound, a mark of the same shape and color."

---

[1] *Tygodnik Lakarski*, 1863, p. 81, a Polish journal ; also in his " Midwifery," in the Polish language, pp. 480–482, Warsaw, 1874.

Dr. William T. Taylor reports the following case :[1] "Mrs. McV—— was delivered on November 30th, 1881, of a female child, upon whose brow was a nævus or varicose aneurism, which projected out between the eyes to the size of a cherry, and assumed a purplish hue whenever the child cried. I inquired of the mother if she had been frightened during her pregnancy. She replied, 'No,' but she told me that *her own mother* had a cancerous tumor on her brow between the eyes, which Dr. Willard Parker, of New York, was treating, and that she had visited her in the early part of her pregnancy, when she was frequently looking at this tumor with painful anxiety, and was much worried about it. I am removing it by pressure with the half of a leaden bullet (referring to the child's nævus)."

Malebranche is the authority for the following case :[2] It is that of a woman in Paris who witnessed a criminal broken upon the wheel when she was two months advanced in pregnancy. She was of "a tender habit of body, and though led by curiosity to this horrid spectacle, very easily moved to pity and compassion. She felt, there-

---

[1] *Phila. Med. Times*, vol. xxii., p. 307.

[2] Goldsmith's "History of the Earth and Animated Nature."

fore, all those strong emotions which so terrible a sight must naturally inspire ; shuddered at every blow the criminal received, and almost swooned at his cries." On her return, and for some days she was in a downcast state, and " her imagination still wrought upon by the spectacle she had lately seen. After some time she seemed perfectly recovered from her fright, and had almost forgotten her former uneasiness. When the time of her delivery approached, she seemed no ways mindful of her former terrors, nor were her pains in labor more than usual in such circumstances. But what was the amazement of her friends and assistants when the child came into the world ! It was found that every limb in its body was broken like those of the malefactor and just in the same place. This poor infant, that had suffered the pains of life even before its coming into the world, did not die, but lived in a hospital in Paris for twenty years after, a wretched instance of the power of the mother in altering and distorting the infant in the womb."

One of the most remarkable cases on record is that of Robert H. Copeland, the snake man.[1]

---

[1] First published in the *Southern Med. and Surg. Jour.*, vol. iii., p. 381, and copied in the *Boston Med. and Surg. Jour.*, vol. xx., p. 98.

The names of **six physicians** are attached to the account, certifying that it is substantially true. When Copeland's mother was six months pregnant, she was struck, but not bitten, by a rattlesnake. She was certain that her child would be deformed from it. She was not mistaken ; it resulted in his being one of the most remarkable curiosities ever seen. For the details, we refer the reader to the original article, at the time of which writing he was twenty-six years old. This case may have suggested, consciously or unconsciously, the character of Elsie Venner, delineated by Dr. Oliver Wendell Holmes in his fascinating novel of that name.

Dr. Ashburton Thompson reports the following case :[1] A mother received at her door a visitor who had in the median line of his neck an aperture where a tracheal tube could be worn—in fact, it was a cleft left by such a tube. The mother was impressed with the conviction that her child would be deformed, and it was born with a cleft in the median line of its neck, almost identical in appearance with the observation.

The same author reports another case, in which

---

[1] Trans. Obstet. Soc., London, vol. xix., p. 94.

the mother received during the same pregnancy two impressions at different times, and differing entirely in their nature. Her child was born with two distinct deformities, corresponding with the separate impressions received.

Dr. F. C. Herr[1] reports the following case : " A lady six weeks advanced in pregnancy was sued before a justice of the peace by her servant-girl for non-payment of her wages. The lady received a notice to appear at the office of the justice. This was a new experience to her, and, as she herself stated, it almost frightened her to death. She went. The justice, whom I know, has a cleft palate. His articulation is most difficult to understand, and his manner of speech, when you do not know him, rather repulsive. After returning home from his office, for weeks this experience was on her mind, and she said she could hear the squire talk all the time. A child was born to her, and the physical conformation of the palate, arches, and roof of the mouth was the counterpart of that of the justice's."

Dr. E. H. Addenbrooke relates the following instances of congenital facial paralysis, caused by

---

[1] *N. Y. Med. Record*, Nov. 28th, 1891.

maternal impressions :[1] " A few weeks since,
while attending Miss B——, I noticed that her
mother suffered from paralysis of the muscles of
the left side of the face. Mrs. B—— informed
me that the affection was congenital, and gave me
the following history : Her mother and her mother's sister (both of them pregnant) were staying
with Mrs. B——'s grandmother, nursing her in
her last illness. One night, as they were assisting her to move, the old lady was suddenly seized
with hemiplegia, the facial paralysis being spe-
cially noticed by them. Both daughters were
confined three or four months afterward, and
each of the children suffered from congenital
facial paralysis of the left side. Mrs. B—— tells
me she has often seen her cousin, and that she is
afflicted in precisely the same way as herself."

Dr. A. E. Gore, ex-President of the Missouri
State Medical Society, cites the following case :[2]
" I knew a lady who while pregnant was chased by
a pet coon, and, if I remember rightly, the coon
sprang upon her right shoulder. She was much
terrified. When the child was born, over the

[1] *Brit. Med. Jour.*, May 13th, 1871.
[2] *St. Louis Courier Med.*, 1883, vol. x., pp. 193-211.

right shoulder and along the neck it was covered with a hairy growth as much resembling that of a coon as two peas resemble one another.''

This case was reported by **Dr. J. Lewis Smith :**[1] A woman in the first months of her pregnancy was passing along a street when she was accosted by a beggar, who raised her hand, *destitute of thumb and fingers*, and in '' God's name'' asked for alms. The woman passed on, but reflecting in whose name money was asked, felt that she had committed a great sin in refusing assistance. She returned to the place where she had met the beggar, but never afterward saw her. Harassed by the thought of an imaginary sin, so that for weeks, according to her statement, she was made wretched by it, she approached her confinement. A female infant was born, otherwise perfect, but lacking the *fingers and thumb* of one hand. The deformed limb seemed to the mother to resemble precisely that of the beggar.

Dr. Minot reports the following case :[2] A respectable married woman, early in her second pregnancy, while riding in a street car observed

---

[1] In his work on '' Diseases of Infancy and Childhood,'' p. 19.

[2] *Boston Med. and Surg. Jour.*, 1870, vol. lxxxiii., p. 344.

a man sitting opposite who had lost all the fingers
of one of his hands. She afterward related the
circumstance to a lady (who reported the facts to
Dr. Minot), saying she feared her child would be
deformed. The child, born at the full period, and
healthy, had no fingers on one of its hands, the
thumb alone being perfect, thus exactly resembling the mutilated hand the mother had seen.

Dr. Fearn cites the following case :[1] A mother
witnessed the removal of one of the bones (meta-
carpal) from her husband's hand, which greatly
shocked and alarmed her. A short time after, she
had a child who was born without the corresponding bone which was removed from the father.

Dr. Dorsey reported the following case :[2] Dr.
G—— sustained a fracture of his leg midway between the ankle and knee. His wife was about
five months advanced in pregnancy. When the
child of which she was pregnant was born, it had
on the leg, corresponding with the injured limb
of the father, and at precisely the same spot, the
appearance of a fracture of a limb, and there was
also a decided shattering of the leg.

---

[1] Report of the Medical Association of Alabama, 1850.
[2] Trans. Med. Association, Ala., 1850.

Fordyce Barker cites a case[1] where a child was born with holes in the lobules of its ears, as a result of the mother seeing holes in the ears of her favorite daughter. The mother was adverse to the daughter having her ears pierced, and it made a decided impression on her, though she had no idea her baby would be so born.

Dr. Bryden[2] cites a case where the mother had seen a picture of a child without a neck, which greatly impressed her. At the time, she was two months pregnant. When the child was born there was no neck.

Purefoy[3] reports the case of a woman who, when about four months pregnant, tried to rear a calf by hand, of which the right ear, right eye, and forelegs were absent. When the child was born, it was similarly deformed—*i.e.*, right ear, right eye, and right arm were wanting.

Roth[4] gives ten cases of hare-lip, one case of spina bifida, one case of cleft palate and one case of nævus resulting from the mother in each in-

---

[1] *Trans. Am. Gynæcol. Soc.*, 1886.
[2] *Brit. Med. Jour.*, July 17th, 1886.
[3] *Med. and Surg. Reporter*, May 31st, 1881.
[4] *Virchow's Archiv.*, Band xci., Heft 3.

stance being impressed with the sight of similar deformities. The time varied from the second or third month till well on in pregnancy.

Cases in which the Child was Affected Physically due to Mental Impressions of the Mother, Resulting from Pure Imagination.

Dalton cited the following case :[1] The wife of a janitor of the College of Physicians and Surgeons, New York, during her pregnancy dreamed that she saw a man who had lost a part of the external ear. This dream made a *great impression*, and she talked of it to her friends. The child was born with one ear, exactly like the defective ear she had seen in her dream. Dr. W. A. Hammond saw it, and says it looked "as if a portion had been cut off with a sharp knife."

Dr. Bryden[2] cites the following case : A mother when three months pregnant dreamed her big toe was bitten off by a rat. When the child was born one big toe was missing.

---

[1] *N. Y. Jour. of Psych. Med.*, vol. ii., p. 19.
[2] *Brit. Med. Jour.*, March 6th, 1886,

Dr. **Maugh** reports the following case :[1] A woman dreamed her child would be a hermaphrodite, of which she informed her husband at the time. When the child was born it was a hermaphrodite.

Dr. **Goodell** reports the following case :[2] A mother was greatly excited by her husband's account of a circumcision in which he had taken part. The mother at the time was two months pregnant ; she was greatly impressed at the time. When the child was born it had no prepuce, but there was a granulating surface like a recent circumcision.

Millingen says :[3] " I know a lady who during her pregnancy was struck with the unpleasant view of leeches applied to a relative's foot. Her child was born with the mark of a leech coiled up in the act of suction on the identical spot."

Besides those cases included in the list, one case each is given by the following physicians, where the mother in the case did not see the deformity, but merely heard of it, the deformity in the

---

[1] *St. Louis Med. and Surg. Jour.*, December, 1882.

[2] *Amer. Jour. Obstetrics*, May, 1871

[3] "Curiosities of Medical Experience," London, vol. ii., p. 273.

child corresponding to that which caused the impression : **Dr. Jasper Cargill,**[1] **Dr. Crickmay,**[2] **Dr. Augustus Hess.**[3]

Cases in which the Child was Affected during Lactation, owing to the Mother's unusual Mental or Physical State.

That the milk is affected by mental impressions is held by nearly all physiologists, among which may be mentioned **Boerhaave,**[4] **Bracket,**[5] **Bonchut,**[6] **Donné,**[7] **Carpenter,**[8] **Hammond,**[9] **Seguin,**[10] **Vernois** and **Becquerel.**[11]

---

[1] *Brit. Med. Jour.*, November 3d, 1877.

[2] *Ibid.*, May 29th, 1886.   [3] *Ibid.*, September 1st, 1877.

[4] Van Swieten, Commentaria, etc., T. iii., p. 403.

[5] " Mémoire sur les Causes des Convulsions chez les Enfans," etc., Paris, 1824, p. 194.

[6] " Hygiène de la Première Enfance," etc., Paris, 1862, p. 177.

[7] " Conseils aux Familles sur la Manière d'élever les Enfans," etc., Paris, 1864, p. 15.

[8] "Cyclopedia of Anatomy and Physiology," vol. iv., part 1, art. Secretion, p. 465.

[9] " Influence of the Maternal Mind over the Offspring during Pregnancy and Lactation," in the New York *Jour. of Psych. Med.*, 1868, p. 23.

[10] " Idiocy and its Treatment by the Physiological Method," New York, 1866, p. 300.

[11] " Du Lait chez la Femme dans l'état de Santé et dans l'état de Maladie," Paris, 1853, p. 73.

Two or three cases will be sufficient to show the results in the child from the mother's being in an unusual mental or physical state during lactation.

Bracket, in his work, mentions the case of a child who was seized with violent convulsions in consequence of taking the milk of a nurse, who had a short time previously experienced intense anger against a woman who had injured her.

Bonchut, in his work, quotes from **Petit-Radel** the case of a child who was attacked with convulsions after being nursed by a woman who had been severely whipped for some trivial fault. He also refers to the instance of a woman who, much excited by the danger which her husband incurred during a quarrel with a soldier, who was about to use his sword, gave her breast, a short time afterward, to her child, aged eleven months and in good health. The infant took a few mouthfuls of her milk, was seized immediately with trembling and panting, and died in a few minutes.

An equally striking case is quoted from the thesis of **Dr. Contesse,** in which " a lady, subject to violent fits of anger, had nursed ten of her children, all of whom had gone into decline and died at different ages. The eleventh was nursed by another woman, and was endowed with excellent health.''

Hammond[1] says : '' Medical men who practise among the poor have noticed that the apprehension felt in regard to a drunken husband will often arrest the secretion of milk.''

Seguin[2] relates several cases, one of which is as follows : '' Mrs. B—— came out overheated from a ball-room, gave the breast to her baby three months old ; he was taken with spasms two hours after, and since is a confirmed idiot and epileptic.''

Many other cases are on record, for which we refer the reader to **Casper's '' Wochenschrift,'' Carpenter's '' Cyclopædia of Anatomy and Physiology,'' Seguin's** work on '' Idiocy and its Treatment by Physiological Method,'' and others *ad lib.*

The Offspring of Animals Affected by Prenatal Influence.

Dareste[3] made experiments with over nine thousand eggs of chickens, producing at will many

---

[1] *Psych. Jour.*, vol. ii., 1868, p. 27.

[2] In his book on Idiocy, etc., p. 300.

[3] '' Comptes Rendus,'' November 3, 1873.

deformities, thus proving beyond doubt that external influences *do affect the development of the embryo*.

M. A. de Frarière[1] gives many interesting cases where peculiar characteristics in animals have been due to influence on the mothers during gestation, and he holds himself personally responsible for any case he gives. He says : " In Egypt, where they are in the habit of hatching chickens in ovens, without the assistance of hens, the pullets brought up in this way show no disposition to brood ; they even lose the desire entirely. Now every one knows the passion with which our hens acquit themselves of that duty.

" An amateur, who was at the same time an excellent observer, assured me that the best methods of obtaining dogs and cats of a gentle disposition was to avoid irritating the mother during gestation ; that it was necessary, on the contrary, to keep her in good humor, and that in exercising her intelligence one could, to a wonderful extent, prepare the young ones to practise those grace-

---

[1] " Education Anterieure ; Influences Maternelles pendant la Gestation sur les Predispositions Morales et Intellectuelles des Enfants," Paris.

ful gambols and pretty tricks which make those animals so amusing."

M. de Frarière goes on to give cases among dogs where the puppies, from mothers who had been tied up, worried and teased, were so vicious that they had to be killed ; while the puppies born prior to this treatment were perfectly docile and good-dispositioned. To use his own expression, when they grew up they were "as gentle as lambs ;" although they were of the largest species of the canine race.

Until several years ago it was customary among stock-breeders to use an inferior horse as a teaser, but owing to the unfavorable results produced on the progeny, it has been entirely abandoned. Cases where this has so resulted will be found among those in the list. The Arabs firmly believe in the influence of the character of the mare upon her foal. They take care to keep her in good condition during the entire period of her gestation, and are persuaded that race alone is not sufficient to insure a foal endowed with the qualities which they value most highly.

———

From these cases we gather that the fœtus may be affected mentally, or physically as well as mentally, by the mental impressions of the mother ; that it may be affected physically through physical impressions on the mother ; that it may be affected physically through mental impressions of the mother ; that to produce either mental or physical impressions on the fœtus the mother need not be affected physically, nor even see the object that causes the impression, but need only have it in mind—*e.g.*, thinking, dreaming, or hearing of it ; that the child may be affected physically and mentally during lactation, due to the mother's unusual state ; and, lastly, that the lower animals are subject to this same pre-natal influence.

We have seen cases where the child has been affected physically as well as mentally even within a short time before birth. These impressions have produced not only superficial results, like those from burns, etc., but those more deeply seated, in which the child has been actually deformed in body and mind. We have even seen cases where, owing to unusually strong impressions, the child has soon after been delivered dead. More than this, it is not only one organ or part that may be affected, but several, or the entire body and mind may be affected ; there may be an over-development or an under-development, depending entirely upon the nature and extent of the impressions.

We have seen cases where the child has been affected by different impressions at different times, the effect being similar to the cause in each case ; and, more than this, impressions can result from causes dating back before pregnancy.

The impression may be prolonged or instantaneous, although prolonged impressions and those constantly repeated are productive of correspondingly greater results.

That the mother has an influence over the mental characteristics of the child, is undoubtedly true. The reason that instances are not more glaringly frequent is obvious. The bodily defect is apparent at the birth of the child ; the mental defect, peculiarity, or whatever it may be, is obvious only at a later period, and by that time the various causes of mental distress, of mental work or of the mental states, whatever they have been during the gestation of that child, have probably been forgotten ; so that while it may be said there are few, none at all, perhaps, who are not more or less affected by pre-natal influence, there are necessarily few whose peculiarities, tendencies, and idiosyncrasies can be accounted for.

As to how the impressions are conveyed to the child, we must confess it is a matter of doubt. Many claim that it is through the blood ; others that it is through the nerves, and again many claim that it is by means of both. The latter would appear to be most correct ; for are there not cases where impressions are wrought on the fœtus too quickly to be carried by the blood ? Certain it is, that by whatever means the impressions are conveyed, the fœtus is undoubtedly influenced through the mother ; and whether or not we know the physiology of it, is it not incumbent on us to advise the adoption of measures during gestation that will insure the future well-being of the child ? Because we do not know how a certain disease is conveyed to an organism, are we to say that we should not treat it ?

We know what a wonderful influence the emotions have over the mind and body. Fear brings out a perspiration on the body and brow of man, causes diarrhœa and urinary secretions ; the hair turns white in a few hours from great fright ; and sorrow and joy are both said to kill. We know what a great influence the passions of anger, hatred, desire, and love have upon the animal economy. Not only do these mental conditions exert a marked influence over the animal organs, but that impress extends to fluids already secret-ed and lying *in situ.*

Thus may also be accounted for the influence of the mother's state over the child during lacta-tion. We have seen cases where this was most marked—*e.g.,* children have become idiots, have even died, or have been otherwise seriously affect-ed by nursing soon after strong mental emotion of the mother. It would seem from such cases that fits of anger, grief, anxiety or a continual fretfulness tend to render the milk thin and serous, and to impart to it qualities which pro-duce intestinal irritation, griping and fever in the child that ingests it.

From the facts before us, the following conclu-sions are warranted :

1. There is no doubt as to pre-natal influence.

2. The child may be affected mentally at any time during pregnancy, but principally during the latter months.

3. The child may be affected physically at any time during pregnancy, but principally during the earlier months.

4. The child can be affected mentally or physi-cally without the mother being aware of it.

5. The child can be affected during the period of lactation by nursing soon after an abnormal physical or mental state of the mother.

6. The lower animals, as well as mankind, are subject to pre-natal influence.

7. To produce an effect on the fœtus the impression may be either instantaneous or prolonged ; but the latter are generally productive of more pronounced results.

8. It is the duty of every physician to advise his patients to guard against the evil consequences of those states on the part of the mother during pregnancy that are injurious to the child, and especially to advise her what measures to adopt to insure the future well-being of her child physically, mentally and morally.

For reference, we refer to several hundred cases carefully selected from medical literature.

LIST OF PUBLISHED CASES
Recorded by Physicians.

Adams, *Amer. Jour. Med. Sci.*, April, 1853.

Aristotle, " De Animalibus Historiæ," Græiè et Latinè, edit. Jo. Gott. Schneider, Lib. vii., et Lib. x., 8vo, Lipsiæ, 1811.

Atkinson, W. B., *Phila. Med. Times,* August 8th, 1874.

Atlee, W. L., *Phila. Med. Times,* 1873–74, vol. iv., p. 715.

Atwell, H. Courtenay, *Quart. Jour. Psych. Med.,* New York, 1868, vol. ii., pp. 322–24.

Bailey, F. K., *Med. and Surg. Rep.,* Philadelphia, 1873, vol. xxvii., p. 420 (four cases).

Baker, C. Q., *Obstet. Gaz.,* Cincinnati, 1878–79, p. 347 (two cases).

Ball, Brayton, Trans. Am. Gynæcol. Soc., 1886.

Ballantyne, J. W., *Edin. Med. Jour.,* 1890–91, pp. 624–35 (four cases).

Ballard, Trans. Lond. Obstet. Soc., vol. vii., 1865.

Barker, Fordyce, Trans. Am. Gynæcol. Soc., 1886, p. 161 (several cases).

Barrett, *Brit. Med. Jour.,* April 10th, 1886.

Baskett, N. M., *St. Louis Cour. Med.,* 1883, pp. 193–211.

Bayard, " Annals Medico-Psychological," 1851, p. 478.

Beale, J. S., *Lancet,* London, 1863, vol. ii.

Beehinger, of Para, Brazil, Annals of Gynæcol., May, 1888.

Blundell, J., in his " Principles and Practice of Obstetrics," p. 99, *et seq.*

Bodenhamer, William, *Med. Record,* New York, March 19th, 1892 (several cases).

Bolton, J. B., *St. Louis Med. and Surg. Jour.,* 1881, vol. xli., p. 437 (three cases).

Brunner, F. R., *Med. and Surg. Rep.,* Philadelphia, 1881, vol. xlv., p. 278 (three cases).

Buck, F. J., *Phila. Med. Times,* 1873–74, vol. iv., p. 715.

Buckel, C. A., *Pacific Med. Jour.,* San Francisco, 1890, p. 65.

Burchman, *Med. and Surg. Rep.,* July 30th, 1881.

Busey, Gynæcol. Trans., 1886.

Cargill, J. E., *Brit. Med. Jour.,* 1877, November 3, p. 655.

Carter, *Brit. Med. Jour.,* July 28th, 1877, p. 96.

Carter, Robert B., in his work " Pathology and Treatment of Hysteria."

Channing, *Amer. Jour. Med. Sci.,* vol. xxv., p. 360.

Chapman, Charles W., *Lancet,* London, October 11th, 1890, p. 951 (two cases).

Child, *Lancet,* London, November 7th, 1868.

Clapperton, *Obstet. Jour. of Great Britain and Ireland,* vol. ii., p. 423.

Coles, *St. Louis Med. and Surg. Jour.,* 1881, p. 161.

Coryder, *Boston Med. and Surg. Jour.,* October, 1874.

Crisp, Trans. Lond. Med. Soc., 1853.

Dabney, Keatings' " Encyclopædia of Children's Diseases," Philadelphia, 1890.

Daly, F. H., *Lancet,* London, 1869, p. 110.

Davis, J., *Med. and Surg. Rep.,* Philadelphia, 1881, p. 80 (two cases).

Davis, R., *Lancet,* London, 1850, p. 466.

Dearsley, H. H., *Lancet,* London, 1885, vol. i., p. 290.

Delacaux, quoted by **Hammond,** *Quart. Jour. Psych. Med.,* January, 1868.

Dewey, *St. Louis Med. and Surg. Jour.,* 1881.

Dickinson, *St. Louis Med. and Surg. Jour.,* 1881, p. 160.

Dotty, L. L., *Med. and Surg. Rep.,* Philadelphia, 1881, p. 26.

Drzewiecki, J., of Warsaw, Poland, *Med. Record,* October 31st, 1891, p. 529 (eight cases).

Dunston, William, *Med. Age,* February 25th, 1889, p. 79.

Elliotson, Elliotson's " Physiology" (several cases).

Fairbrother, *St. Louis Med. and Surg. Jour.*, 1881, p. 164.

Fearn, R. Lee, *Am. Jour. Med. Sci.*, Philadelphia., vol. xxv., p. 359.

Fearn, Trans. Alabama Med. Assoc., 1850.

Furman, *St. Louis Med. and Surg. Jour.*, May 5th, 1880.

Goodell, *Amer. Jour. of Obstet.*, May, 1871, p. 131.

Graham, F., *Brit. Med. Jour.*, March 6th, 1886.

Graham, T. H., M.R.C.S., *Brit. Med. Jour.*, London, 1868, p. 51.

Griffith, *Lancet*, London, November 3d, 1887.

Hailey, Hammet, F.L.S., Trans. Obstet. Soc., London, 1865.

Haldeman, J. S., *Phila. Med. Times*, 1882--83, p. 763.

Hammond, William A., *Quart. Jour. Psych. Med.*, New York, 1868, vol. ii., pp. 1-28 (seventeen cases).

Hayward, *Amer. Jour. Med. Sci.*, vol. xxv., p. 359.

Heddens, W. J., *Amer. Jour. Med. Sci.*, vol xxiii., p. 558.

Herr, F. C., *Med. Record*, October 31st, 1891 p. 659.

Hess, Augustus, *Brit. Med. Jour.*, August 25th, 1877, p. 282.

Hill, J. L., *Med. and Surg. Rep.*, January 27th, 1877 (six cases).

Hoare, J., M.R.C.S., *Lancet*, London, 1831–32, p. 441.

Hope, W. T., *Virg. Med. Month.*, 1879–80, p. 882.

Huntley, *Brit. Med Jour.*, March 13th, 1875.

Jackson, *Amer. Jour. Med. Sci.*, vol. xxv., p. 358.

Jackson, Trans. Med. Soc. Pa., Philadelphia, 1867–68, vol. xl., p. 665.

Jameson, *Amer. Pract.*, vol. xviii., p. 76.

Jenkins, J., C.B., *Lancet*, London, 1876, vol. ii., p. 851.

Johnston, B. R., *Brit. Med. Jour.*, March 28th, 1885.

Kerr, *Amer. Jour. Med. Sci.*, July, 1857, p. 285.

Kesteven, W. B., *Med. Times*, London, 1842–43, vol. vii., p. 126.

Kline, H. D., *Toledo Med. and Surg. Rep.*, 1891, vol. iv., pp. 28–31.

Le Crone, L. W., *Med. Age*, April 25th, 1889, p. 178.

Lee, R. J., F.R.C.P., *Brit. Med. Jour.*, London, 1875, p. 167.

Lee, R. J., *Lancet*, London, 1877, p. 651.

Leeson, T. R., M.R.C.S., L.M.D., *Brit. Med. Jour.*, London, 1874, p. 502.

Leonard, R. A., *Med. Jour. and Exam.*, Chicago, 1881, p. 87.

Liégey, *Jour. de Méd. Chir. et Pharm.*, October, 1880.

Lowman, W. R., *Med. Record*, August 17th, 1889, p. 176.

Lowrie, J. O., *Med. Age*, March 11th, 1889, p. 108 (twenty cases).

Lutz, *St. Louis Med. and Surg. Jour.*, 1881, p. 170.

Mackay, H. M., *Canada Lancet*, Toronto, 1878, p. 234 (two cases).

Magill, Trans. Med. Soc. Pa., Philadelphia, 1876–77, vol. xl., p. 665.

Martin, T., *Amer. Jour. Med. Sci.*

Martyn, William, Trans. Obstet. Soc., London, vol. vii., 1865.

Maugh, *St. Louis Med. and Surg. Jour.*, 1882, vol. xliii., pp. 596–615 (five cases).

Mauriceau, Mauriceau's work, 2d ed., 1716, Chamberlin, chap. entitled "Of the Diseases of Women with Child."

Meadows, Alfred, M.R.C.P., Trans. Obstet. Soc., London, 1865.

Middleton, W. J., *Med. Record,* February 22d, 1890, p. 226.

Miller, Charles H., *Med. and Surg. Rep.,* Philadelphia, 1881, p. 80 (five cases).

Miller, Charles H., *The Southern Clinic,* Richmond, 1883, pp. 95–100 (eight cases).

Miller, Charles H., *Obstet. Gaz.,* Cincinnati, vol. iv., pp. 65–68.

Mitchell, Sir Arthur, Trans. Obstet. Soc., London, vol. xxvi., p. 127 (several cases).

Mitchell, L. B., *Med. Age,* April 25th, 1889, p. 179.

Montgomery, " Signs and Symptoms of Pregnancy," 1857, pp. 35–36 (several cases).

Nichols, Thomas B., *Med. Age,* December 10th, 1888, p. 537.

O'Reilly, J. H., *Med. Herald,* Louisville, 1883–84, pp. 160–182 (eight cases).

Paget, Sir James, quoted by T. Smith, *Lancet,* London, August 16th, 1867.

Palmer, B. N., *Med. Age,* April 25th, 1889, p. 180.

Parker, Gynæcol. Trans., 1886.

Parker, *Amer. Jour. Med. Sci.,* vol. xxv., p. 360.

Phila. Med. Times, December 2d, 1882 (case from the editor)

Pinel, Philip, " Traité Medico-Philosophique sur l'Aliénation Mentale," 2d ed., 8vo, Paris, 1809.

Plinius, Caius Secundus, " Natura Historiarum," Floio Hagæ, 1518.

Prentiss, D. Webster, *Phila. Med. Times,* vol. xii., p. 385.

Ramsey, D. W., *Med. Brief,* St. Louis, 1880, vol. viii., p. 462.

Rawlins, James S., *Med. and Surg. Rep.,* Philadelphia, 1881, vol. xliv., p. 671.

Reamy, Thaddeus A., *Amer. Jour. Obstet.,* vol. i., 1878, p. 634.

Robinson, J. A., Trans. Amer. Gynæcol. Soc., vol. ii., 1886, p. 175.

Rowland, *St. Louis Med. and Surg. Jour.,* 1881, pp. 174–75 (two cases).

Rush, Benjamin, " Medical Inquiries and Observations," etc., 8vo, Philadelphia, 1789.

Saunder, T. D., *Brit. Med. Jour.,* March 24th, 1877, p. 376.

Scott, *St. Louis Med. and Surg. Jour.,* 1882, vol. xliii., p. 620.

Sedgwick, Proceedings Royal Med. and Chir. Soc., London, vol. viii.

Seguin, E., *Phila. Med. Times,* 1876–77, vol. vii., pp. 121–23 (ten cases).

Shaw, T. H., Trans. Amer. Gynæcol. Soc., vol. ii., 1886, p. 175

Shoreland, George, *Lancet*, London, 1850, p. 466.

Slusser, L., *Med. Exam.* and *Phila. Med. Times*, 1876–77, vol. vii.

Smith, Heywood, *Med. and Surg. Rep.*, May 31st, 1881.

Smith, T., *Lancet*, London, August 17th, 1867.

Smith, T. J., Trans. Med. Soc. N. J., Newark, 1878, p. 278 (two cases).

Smyth, W., *Brit. Med. Jour.*, July 14th, 1877, p. 67.

Southard, Trans. Med. Soc. N. J., Newark, 1871, p. 188 (three cases).

Spitzka, in his work on " Insanity ;" also in *Med. Cla.*, p. 35, 1888 (several cases).

Stedman, T. L., *Med. Record*, New York, January 1st, 1887 (twelve cases).

Stevens, *Obstet. Gaz.*, vol. iii., p. 465.

Stewart, Gynæcol. Trans., 1886.

Stewart, *Amer. Jour. Obstet.*, vol. vi., p. 641.

Stockard, C. C., *St. Louis Med. and Surg. Jour.*, 1881, vol. xii., p. 101 (four cases).

Storer, *Amer. Jour. Med. Sci.*, vol. xxv.. p. 356.

Stubbs, *Phila. Med. Times*, 1873–74, vol. iv., p. 715.

Swift, *New York Med. Jour.*, October 9th, 1886.

Taylor, *Amer. Jour. Obstet.*, vol. vi., p. 641, or *Obstet. Gaz.*, vol. iv., p. 67.

Taylor, William T., *Phila. Med. Times*, 1882–83, vol. xiii., p. 155.

Taylor, William T., *Phila. Med. Times*, 1876–77, vol. vii., pp. 73–75 (fourteen cases).

Thompson, C. M., *Brit. Med. Jour.*, London, 1874, p. 469 (three cases).

Thompson, Trans. Obstet. Soc., London, 1877.

Toland, H. H., *Pacific Med. and Surg. Jour.*, San Francisco, 1862–63, vol. ii., pp. 297–301 (six cases).

Trenholme, *St. Louis Med. and Surg. Jour.*, May 5th, 1880 (quoted two cases).

Tuke. in his work '' Influence of the Mind upon the Body'' (several cases).

Vatin, H. D., *Chicago Med. Jour. and Exam.*, 1881, p. 87.

Wall, *Med. Record*, New York, 1881.

Watson, J. M., *Nashville Med. and Surgical Jour.*, 1860, vol. xviii., pp. 97–109.

Weller, *Chicago Med. Jour. and Exam.*, 1881, vol. xliii., p. 87 (two cases).

Wendell, *Louisville Med. News* (two cases).

Wetherley, J., *Med. Record*, September 21st, 1889, p. 316 (six cases).

Whitelaw, M., *Brit. Med. Jour.,* July 14th, 1877, p. 36 (two cases).

Whittle, G., *Brit. Med. Jour.,* October 5th, 1878, p. 543.

Wilson, *Obstet. Jour. Gt. Brit. and Ire.,* vol. viii., p. 333.

Wood, W. J. H., *Brit. Med. Jour.,* August 26th, 1876, p. 270.

Wright, C. O., *Cincinnati Lancet and Observer.*

Wright, *Amer. Jour. Obstet.,* January, 1878.

CHAPTER III.

Cases (continued).

"'Tis strange—but true ; for truth is always strange,
Stranger than fiction."
—Byron.

THE following cases, carefully selected from well-known authors, from prominent physicians and from my own practice—I would here say that I can vouch for the cases I have myself reported —will illustrate how the laws of pre-natal influence may be taken advantage of to better future generations. For if the body and mind can be so greatly changed, warped or influenced in one way, as shown in the preceding chapter, so it can be in another. If one impression can be photographed, as it were, on a child's mind, so can another ; and so intellectual power, good physique and a worthy disposition may be imparted to the offspring.

Mental Development and Special Talent.

In the parents' mode of life necessary to transmit intellectual ability or talent through pre-natal influence, much might be learned from the circumstances which preceded the birth of men gifted with special abilities, had we any record of such conditions. This record is wanting in most instances, but there are some cases which convey a good idea of how pre-natal influence may be applied to benefit the child.

Napoleon Bonaparte.—During the months preceding Napoleon's birth, his mother was surrounded with scenes of battle—skirmishes, quick marches. She accompanied her husband on horseback upon a military campaign, and, moreover, deeply interested herself in strategy and the arts of war. She thus conferred upon her son a love of conquest and a military genius before which all Europe trembled for many years.

While Napoleon was still a mere child, he displayed a remarkable taste for war. He was constantly talking of it and anxiously looking forward to the time when he could enter upon a military life. When he was only a few years old he used to delight in thunder storms ; he loved to see the lightning and hear the peals of thunder. So strong was this tendency that sometimes it was impossible to induce him to seek shelter during a storm, instead of which he would expose himself to the elements to delight in their fury. Although he had four brothers, none of them ever displayed any marked military ability, nor, while young, any fondness for war.

Burns.—The mother of Robert Burns was of cheerful disposition, though in humble and often pinching circumstances. She had an excellent memory for old songs and ballads, and she sang them constantly as she went about her household duties. By the constant exercise of this order of mental faculties she conferred upon her eldest son a degree of ability which she herself did not possess.

Poetical Talent.—The following case, as given by **Dr. F. W. Moffatt** in a letter to the editor of the *Medical Record*, and published in that journal February 13th, 1892, we quote. It was given in the mother's own words, who, by the way, was the mother of the authoress of that well-known French novel " Mal Moulée" :

" When I was pregnant with my third child I put my whole energies to bring forth a poet. I read poetry, doted on it, lived in it, and when, during the day, unable to read it, thought of it, and when asleep dreamed of it. Byron being my favorite poet, I devoted to him more than a due proportion of my reading. My daughter is now a poetess, and her poems partake so much of Byron's style that her critics have often asked her why she did not sometimes select another model." This mother goes on to say : " When next I became pregnant, my desires had been satisfied and I did not care what the child would become. The result is that he has no strong qualities." Dr. Moffatt cites several other cases which will be referred to later on.

For this case we are indebted to the author of " Husband and Wife" :

" A teacher in a Western State had under her instruction five children belonging to one family. " The two eldest were dull, inert and slow to learn ; while the third, a girl about twelve years of age, was remarkably bright, sensitive and talented. Not only apt and quick at her lessons, she possessed a fine poetic temperament, accompanied by a keen appreciation of the beauties of nature ; she could also write a theme in prose or verse with ease and facility. The children younger than this one were both physically and mentally superior to the two eldest, but far inferior to her in talent and refinement of manners." These differences were so marked that the teacher's curiosity was excited to learn the cause. Becoming intimately acquainted with the mother (who at first could assign no reason for the diversity), the teacher at length ascertained the following facts :

Some years prior to the birth of the favored child, the mother (who, though reared in an Eastern State, in the enjoyment of fair advantages, had become the wife of a farmer in a new country, deprived of literary and social privileges, and overworked in the struggle to acquire a competence) had her attention attracted to a volume of Walter Scott's poems, brought to the house by a travelling peddler. She was so seized with a desire to possess and read the book that, not having at hand the money to purchase it, she had walked four miles at night to borrow of a friend a sufficient sum for the purpose. " And a glorious time I had in reading it," she said, " for often in the perusal of its pages I forgot my fatigues and cares." Having read the book so often that she came to know much of it by rote, she used to sing the songs to the child when an infant, and afterward to repeat the stories to her when a little girl. Here, no doubt, was the source of the superior intelligence, refinement and poetic tendencies of the child."

Musical Talent.—M. A. de Frarière gives some interesting cases,[1] and their value is enhanced by his repeated statements that he has related nothing as a fact of which he has not had personal knowledge, and for the accuracy of which he holds himself personally responsible. Among the cases he gives are several illustrating how musical talent has been conferred on the offspring as a result of the mother cultivating this talent in herself during gestation. The first is that of Luigi Ricci, who, on August 15th, 1861, when he was only eight years old, directed the singers at the Basilique de San Guisto, at Trieste, where they performed a mass of his own composition. The church was crowded.

Wolfgang Mozart was another notable instance of latent musical talent, as was also the daughter of Madame Borghi-Mamo. M. de Frarière says that in each of these children their wonderful display of musical genius is accounted for by the mother exercising her musical talents and being surrounded by musical people during her

---

[1] " Education Anterieure ; Influences Maternelles pendant la Gestation sur les Predispositions Morales et Intellectuelles des Enfants." Published at Paris.

pregnancy. He goes on to say that "I learn from the brother of the celebrated Wolfgang, who died at Milan, and who, by the way, *had no disposition* for music, that their mother had cultivated music during the early years of her married life, but that she had afterward abandoned it and even taken a dislike to it after her first two accouchements. Then this brother was born under the latter influence, and he had no musical talent."

In an account of Luigi, written at Boulogne, the writer says, "Every one in the town attributes the precocious musical intelligence of the little Luigi to the exceptional position in which the mother found herself while *enceinte.*"

In regard to the little daughter of Madame Borghi-Mamo, the journal *Le Nord*, November 14th, 1859, contained the following lines: " The little daughter of Madame Borghi-Mamo, three or four years of age, already displays a decided talent for music. It is wonderful to hear this *virtuose en herbe*, who has never received a lesson, as you may imagine, sing from one end to the other the part of Rosine from having heard it practised. She reproduces with her little crystal voice all the turns, all the elegances, and all the most delicate expressions and flourishes. No shade of the impersonation escapes this miniature Rosine. At the time when Madame Borghi-Mamo was *enceinte*, she sang constantly ; she even sang on the very eve of the day on which they could print that mother and child were doing well. She is called Erminia, like the great artiste who is now making the tour of the United States with a voice which is unfailing and an ardor which will only be extinguished with her life."

M. de Frarière has also given examples in which the parent or parents were possessed of marked musical talent, but who had children of no musical ability, as the mother gave no attention to her music during the time she was pregnant.

Dr. F. W. Moffatt, in the letter before referred to, gives the following case, quoted :

" When I was first pregnant, I wished my offspring to be a musician. So, during the period of that pregnancy, I settled my whole mind on music, attended every musical entertainment I possibly could. I had my husband, who has a violin, play for me by the hour. When the child was born, it was a girl, which grew and prospered, and finally became, as you have undoubtedly heard, an expert musician."

Dr. A. B——, a physician of the highest standing, has kindly communicated the following case to us, and as it is that of his own daughter, he wishes his name withheld. We can say that we know two of the daughters, the one who is musical and one of the others, and can vouch for what he has said as to their respective musical talents.

"Mrs. A. B—— had four children, all girls, now grown to womanhood, and all, to some extent, musical. The youngest girl has an unusual talent for music, which is accounted for in the following way : While pregnant with her, her mother paid a visit to her old home. There, owing to a very extensive circle of family connections, many of whom were musical, she was not only a great deal among musical people, but was constantly exercising her own talents."

Dr. Cowan has given the following case :

" Some years ago a man, one of whose hobbies was that unless an individual was a musician there was something radically wrong in his make-up, married a woman who did not know the first elements of music. This woman, his wife, knowing his desire for musical abilities in children and his utter carelessness or want of interest in children who did not possess such, at first had a dread that she would bear a child wanting in his desires.

But she made up her mind that such should not be the case, and to this end she obtained a piano, practised upon it for a certain number of hours daily, and daily cultivated what voice she had in singing. Coupled with this was the strong desire of her whole soul to have a child possessing a genius for music. This mother has now two children, both of which are born musicians. They can sing any tune they once hear, and can already play the most difficult music placed before them. They delight and revel in it."

Here are six instances of marked musical talent due to the influence on the mother during pregnancy. Four of them at least had brothers or sisters born later, when the mother was not exerting her talents in a musical direction, who were entirely lacking in musical genius.

Arithmetical Talent.—Zerah Colburn (born at Cabot, Vt., September 1st, 1804, died March 2d, 1840) was a prodigy in arithmetical calculation. At six years of age he manifested such powers of computation as to astonish the learned world. Questions in multiplication of five places of figures, reduction, rule of three, compound fractions, and obtaining factors of large numbers were answered with accuracy and with marvellous quickness. Among the questions propounded to him on his visit at Harvard College were the following : How many days and hours in 1811 years? His answer, given in twenty seconds, was 661,015 days, 15,864,360 hours. How many seconds in eleven years? The answer, given in four seconds, was 346,896,000. The reason for this remarkable arithmetical talent was that a few months before his birth, his mother, who had never been taught arithmetic, had on her mind for a day and a night a puzzling question as to how many yards of cloth a given amount of yarn which she had would make. To a person understanding arithmetic this would be a simple problem, but she had to do it by a mental process, without rule, and this extraordinary effort on her part was organized in her child and made him a genius in mental arithmetic.

Business Talent.—The following case, known to the author, will show how business ability may be conferred. The family of H—— was an old and distinguished one, yet in all their history there was not one member of it who had any marked business ability, although renown in various professions was attained by many. In the present generation, however, there is one who is possessed of excellent business capacity. This tendency showed itself in early years, and so strong was the latent force that he overcame many obstacles, and is considered a man of some-what unusual business capacity. The reason for this was that his mother, although a most unpractical woman, had her attention constantly divert-ed to business matters of serious importance dur-ing the time she was pregnant with him. Not only was the mother a very unpractical, unbusi-ness-like woman, but the father, as well as a large family of brothers and sisters, were the same to a degree which unfitted them entirely for any posi-tion requiring much business ability.

Mechanical Talent.—Dr. Cowan cites the fol-lowing case :

" A man, who by profession was an engineer and who had just started business on his own ac-count, received a commission from a prominent and wealthy firm to construct a large and peculiar steam-engine. So desirous was he to succeed, and please and satisfy his employers, that he worked whole days and evenings in concentrated study to perfect the design. In doing this, his wife, who was along in pregnancy, got interest-ed, and together they thought, talked and planned. When the time arrived a daughter was born, who, in growing, developed in an unusual degree a talent to invent and construct."

Literary Talent.—In the case of Mrs. R——, personally known to the author, there was manifested early in life considerable literary talent, which took the special direction of dietetics and health reform. This is accounted for by her relatives in the following way : Her father, a physician, during the time her mother was pregnant with her, was engaged in writing lectures on hygienic subjects, and the mother took a great interest in his work, acting the part of home critic and assisting him in every possible way.

The following case is given by **Dr. Moffat,** in the mother's own words :[1] " During the period of my second pregnancy I wished my child to be an editor, and I bent my whole mind to the attainment of such result. I read the papers almost continuously, paying special attention to the leading editorials of such of the great periodicals and dailies of that time as I could lay hands on, even neglecting my household duties in my efforts to attain the desired results." The mother

---

[1] *Med. Record*, February 13th, 1892.

goes on to say that when this child grew up he displayed marked literary talent.

Fondness for Medical and Legal Study.—Dr. S——, Dean of —— Medical College, once told the author that one of his sons was a born doctor, for his mother during gestation devoted much of her attention to medical subjects. Another son takes little interest in medical subjects, but seems naturally adapted to the bar. Dr. S—— further stated that the mother when pregnant with the second son spent much time in studying legal questions.

Physical Development.

The following well-known cases, which appeared in one family, will be found in detail in the New York *Medical Record*, 1891, vol. xl., p. 42, and are reported by **Dr. R. Osgood Mason**, of New York, through **Dr. M. K. Bowers**, of Harrisburg, Pa. The parents of the children were pronounced brunettes ; the grandparents all have dark complexions and dark hair, and the family, as far back as its history can be traced, is entirely free from freaks or abnormalities of any kind. The parents were well educated and unusually intelligent people. The grandfather on the mother's side at present holds a prominent position in one of the offices of the State Government. To these parents was born, as might naturally be expected, a dark-complexioned child. Early in the second pregnancy of the mother, she was surprised and made nervous by the sudden and unexpected appearance of a large beautiful albino rat, sent to her from friends in Philadelphia, to which she afterward became much attached. Before her child was born she predicted that it would be an albino.

She was right ; when it was born it was seen to be a perfect albino, and a beautiful child. The mother became unusually fond of it, and wished that she might have another albino. When she next became pregnant she again predicted that she would have a child similar to the last, and she did all in her power to make it so, keeping the face of her first albino child constantly before her. When the child was born it was seen to be as perfect an albino as the first, but a girl—the first being a boy. It might be well to add here that the rat died before the first child was born.

She again became pregnant, but this time hoped she would have a dark-complexioned child. She was surrounded, though, by the same influences, and the same models were before her. She feared disappointment, and she experienced it. The third child was as perfect an albino as the first. Upon the occurrence of her next pregnancy she was thoroughly aroused, and was extremely anxious to have a dark-complexioned child. She at once sent her albino children away to her mother's house, to remain during her pregnancy. "Her one constant song and desire was for the dark-haired baby. She talked of it constantly—she even talked of it in her sleep." She felt that she would not be disappointed, and she was not. A perfect dark-haired child was born.

Dr. Bowers further states that the whole family are remarkably healthy, and the albinos are much better specimens of that type than any found in museums or circus shows. The hair is snow-white and remarkably fine and soft, the eyebrows and lashes are the same. The eyes and complexion are of perfect albino type.

K. N. Fenwick, A.M., M.D., of Kingston, Ont., says in an article which appeared in the New York *Medical Record*, October 17th, 1891 :

" Being interested in Dr. Mason's article in the *Record* for July 11th, and a firm believer in the influence of maternal impressions on the fœtus in utero, I would like to add my quota to the evidence for this side of the argument.

" Mrs. T. R—— and her husband are both of dark complexion, and their first two children were quite dark, with black hair. During her third pregnancy, she wakened up one morning to find the sky of a peculiar crimson color, which made such a vivid impression that, as she expressed herself, she ' thought it was the judgment day.' At full term she was delivered of an albino boy." This lady had five albino children altogether, besides three dark-complexioned ones. Dr. Fenwick then goes on to give two more cases, which may be found in the same journal. Other albino cases will be found in the list, pp. 53–64.

Dr. Edward Garraway cites the following case :[1]

" A lady of refined taste was in the habit of sitting before a group of statuary, with one little figure of which she was greatly enamored. This was a Cupid reposing, his cheek resting on the back of his hand. When her baby was born, his resemblance in form and feature to the little Cupid

---

[1] *Brit. Med. Jour.*, 1886, vol. i , p. 287 ; also given by Dr. J. Drzewiecki in the New York *Med. Record*, October 31st, 1891, p. 529.

was at once striking.   On seeing him the next day
in his cradle, I perceived he had assumed the precise attitude of the statuette—the cheek upon the
back of the hand ; and this position he invariably,
and of course involuntarily, adopted during sleep
not only throughout infancy, but up to advanced
boyhood, when I lost sight of him."

Dr. Britton cites the following case :

" Some time since, we met with a youth who
had finely moulded limbs and a symmetrical form
throughout.   His mother has a large, lean, at-
tenuated frame, that does not offer so much as a
single suggestion of the beautiful.   The boy is
doubtless indebted for his fine form to the presence
of a beautiful French lithograph in his mother's
sleeping apartment, and which presented for her
contemplation the faultless form of a naked child."

Dr. A. Newton cites the following case :

" A mother at an early stage in pregnancy had
her attention drawn to a beautiful figure of a child
in wax, exhibited in a shop window in one of our
cities.   It had a lovely face, indicative of an amiable character, and it greatly pleased the lady's
fancy.   She frequently visited the spot in order
to feast her eyes upon its pleasing features, and
brought the energies of her soul to bear in an en-

deavor to transfer them to the unfolding germ within. When her child (a daughter) was born, its features were an almost exact copy of those of the beautiful figure, markedly different from the features of any other of the family. There are five other children, none of whom are remarkable for beauty."

Dr. J. Adams, author of " Advice to Mothers," etc., whose wide experience of over forty years has brought him in contact with many cases, has kindly communicated to us the two following instances, as well as one or two others :

" Both Mr. and Mrs. P—— had decidedly dark complexions and hair, and consequently their children partook of the same type. There was, however, one notable exception in their little Mary, who was the opposite in everything, being as fair as a lily, with light yellow hair. The reason for this was that Mrs. P——, while pregnant with her, conceived a great fancy for one of the colored pictures which accompany the Christmas *Illustrated London News*. Having had it framed, she hung it in her bedroom just opposite her bed, so that it was the first object which met her eye when wakening in the morning. The child was strikingly like the picture.

" Mrs. J—— was the mother of several children who were not by any means remarkable for their beauty. She had one child, however, which differed very markedly from the others in this respect. She attributed the beauty of this child to the influence of a beautiful French doll, which had been sent from Paris to one of her children, and which she kept locked up in a drawer for fear of its being destroyed. At this time she was pregnant, and being strongly impressed by the beauty of the doll, she could not refrain from frequently taking a look at it. When her child was born the result was a remarkable resemblance between the child and the doll."

In the two following cases we knew the ladies intimately. They are people of the highest standing, whose veracity is undoubted. The accounts are given in their own words :

" Mrs. A——, her husband, and all her children (with one exception) were quite dark-haired, ordinary-looking people. When she was pregnant with this one, she had at the side of her bed a lovely picture of a little girl with golden curls and dark, violet eyes, with dark lashes and eyebrows. She was constantly looking at the picture and longing that her child might be as beautiful.

When the little one was born, to her great delight the likeness was remarkable. The child grew to be a typical blonde, and so beautiful that artists repeatedly requested her to sit for her picture."

This instance, which occurred in the family of Mrs. B——, is as follows :

" A neighbor living next door to her, who had recently come from the South, and to whom she was an entire stranger, was taken seriously ill. Mrs. B—— took a great interest in her, and was constantly with her during this long sickness. The sick friend at the time of her illness was grieving over the death of a beautiful little girl, which happened some time before the mother was taken sick. In her bedroom was a life-size painting of this child, taken at the age of seven months. Mrs. B—— was pregnant at the time of her new friend's illness, and was very much impressed by the painting of the lovely child, the mother talking almost constantly of it. When Mrs. B——'s baby was born, so great was the likeness that her friend insisted on its being named after her child ; and at the age of seven months the most intimate friends of the family could hardly be convinced that the portrait was not that of the living child. At the present time, although the girl has grown up, she is entirely unlike her own people, and retains a surprising resemblance to the Southern family." The father of the dead girl was still in the South, where he had been living for two years.

Dr. Williams, in the St. Louis *Medical and Surgical Journal* for December, 1881, gives the following case, which was quoted by **Dr. Dewey:**

" A mother had living in her house, both before and during pregnancy, a lady to whom she was *much* attached. This lady's eyes differed in color—one being blue and the other black ; besides, one leg was shorter than the other. When the child was born, it had one eye blue and the other black, and one leg was shorter than the other. The peculiarities of the child and the mother's friend corresponded *exactly.*"

The following case is a most interesting one. I knew all the circumstances, and will repeat that I can vouch for every case I have myself reported. There were several other physicians connected with the case besides myself, who can testify as to every detail in connection with it. Among them were Dr. J. Adams, Dr. C. S. Elliot, Dr. H. C. S. Elliot, and Dr. J. B. Hall. The case is that of a delicate lady, with a particularly weak digestion,

who, when she was five weeks pregnant, was taken
with most violent nausea and vomiting. It seemed
irresistible, and went from bad to worse. After
the first few days, she took to bed, where she
stayed for ten weeks. She was fed artificially, as
everything was rejected from her stomach. When
she was almost given up, she suddenly changed
for the better and recovered sufficiently to sit up.
From this she gradually got about the house
again, although she was never free from indiges-
tion during the entire period of gestation. Owing
to her delicate state of health she was strongly
advised to do everything to insure her child's
future well-being, which she was most anxious to
do, her own words being : " I am determined my
child shall not be a weakling." From this time
until its birth—five months and a half—she lived
only on the simplest kind of food, discarding all
stimulants, tea, coffee, etc. She carried out the
system of bathing, dress and, as far as she could,
the exercising, as recommended in this work, and
did everything in her power to exert a favorable
influence over the child. The result was that
when it was born, instead of being a puny, wail-
ing little sufferer, as many expected, it was strong
and vigorous. The first two months the little one

suffered from colic, owing to some difficulty in
selecting the right food, for her mother was too
delicate to nurse her ; but after that " she was
never sick. She was a perfect sleeper—never
kept the nurse awake one hour at night," and as
she grew older she grew even more sturdy.
When I last saw her she was as perfect a speci-
men of a healthy child as I ever met. Her father,
as well as her mother, is one whose digestion is
naturally weak.

It has been noted that among the Italian peas-
antry, unlettered and uncultured as they are, the
thoughtful features of the Madonna are often
easily recognized in the faces of the children.
Nor is this to be wondered at when it is remembered that almost every religious edifice in that
country is provided with beautiful representations
of the Virgin, and when we recall the intense
adoration of the image which is dominant in the
Italian woman's soul.

Moral Tendencies.

Irreligion.—Mrs. L——, during the time she
was pregnant with her little girl, had a strong
antipathy to all matters pertaining to religion,
which antipathy had developed since becoming

pregnant. She could not be persuaded to read or listen to the teachings of the Bible, and she shunned everything connected with it. Her child, now a girl in her eleventh year, is the exact counterpart of her mother's state of mind during the time she was pregnant. So strong is the child's distaste for religious forms and ideas that it seems overpowering. Her grandmother's own words were: " We have almost given up hope of ever getting her to have anything to do with the Bible."

Inebriety.—Mr. S——, a young man not over twenty-six years of age, whose case the author has followed with interest, is a most hopeless drunkard. His mother and father, though people of fair education and respectable standing, were confirmed drunkards. The mother was constantly in a state of intoxication during her pregnancy with the child. So strong is the craving for alcoholic drinks, and so weak is the power of withstanding temptation in her son, that his case is almost hopeless. Owing to his being left an orphan while only a few weeks of age, some friends adopted him. They thought that by training him to hate liquor, and giving him every educational advantage, he might be saved from the fatal tendency and weakness he inherited. They were, however, doomed to disappointment, in spite of every medical attention and every effort they could put forth. He is now in an inebriate asylum.

Timidity.—One writer cites the two following cases :

" A wife became *enceinte* unintentionally at an unfavorable time. Her husband and herself had planned to erect a new dwelling that season, and in the occupations and bustle incident to this enterprise the interests of the unborn were overlooked. The mother, overburdened with domestic cares and labors, found little opportunity for seclusion and repose, and was continually striving to conceal her state from the rude men—mechanics and laborers—who were employed on the premises. In due time a child was born, but instead of being, as it should have been, a blessing to its parents, it was feeble, extremely irritable, and nervously afraid of strangers. When any person with whom it was not familiar entered the house, it would set up a violent screaming and could not be pacified. As it grew up it continued to manifest the same excessive timidity, often running to hide in the house if a stranger was seen to approach."

An Unsettled Turn of Mind.—"A child well known to the writer was begotten at a time when its parents were about removing to a new location, with a change in business. In due time they were gladdened by the birth of a vigorous and healthy boy. But as he grew up, while in many respects a great source of pleasure to his parents, he developed a propensity for roving about and visiting new places—an indisposition to remain long at any employment or in any locality. When earnestly remonstrated with for this tendency by his parents on one occasion, when about fifteen years of age, he burst out, through a shower of tears, with these significant words : ' Well, I don't know what makes me do so ; but there is something in me which continually says, " Go ! go ! " and I *can't* stay long in any place ! ' These words conveyed to his parents a solution of the whole matter. In the circumstances under which the boy was begotten, the impulse to ' go,' the desire of change, had been infused into the very elements of his being. How could he be expected to do otherwise than act it out ? It should be added that through the efforts of the parents and the boy himself he was able, at the age of twenty-three, to settle down to a useful occupation."

A mother writes : " I read the ' Iliad ' for six months before my child was born, and he is actu-ally like Achilles, so restless that I fear he is ruined for life."

Sensuality.—Dr. William R. Lowman, in an article entitled " Résumé on Maternal Impres-sions," published in the *Medical Record*, August 17th, 1889, says :

" Observers of large experiences with the ille-gitimate[1] say that the mental suffering of the dis-graced mother reacts on the children, arrests de-velopment, produces mental deficiency, or in after years, even though under the best moral care, the offspring oftentimes follows the mother in a life of sin. The sins of the parents shall be visited on the offspring, and this law of impression is the means of transmissal."

While this may be true, it is not absolutely necessary that either of the parents should live what is commonly known as " a life of sin" in order that their children shall lead dissolute lives, as the following case will prove. We have be-sides this case several others of a similar nature ; the facts, however, are not given clearly enough,

---

[1] Mitchel, *Med. Record*, July 16th, 1887.

and there is not sufficient proof to warrant their being printed ; but who cannot recall such cases even among the most moral people ?

Mr. and Mrs. R. M——, most refined people of the highest standing, have a daughter of a perverted sensual nature. The heart-broken mother accounts for it in the same way in which countless numbers of other such unfortunate cases may be explained. She told the writer that she and her husband blamed themselves for it as a result of over-indulgence during pregnancy. The case is all the more deplorable in that the young lady is unusually talented and attractive.

Tendency to Thieving.—The following case, as recorded by a physician, came from the lips of a gentleman whose son had just been committed to State prison. (The names must be withheld.)

" When I was married, I thought that for the first year my wife and I could live more cheaply by remaining with my mother in the old homestead. We did so. My wife was timid and bashful in the presence of her mother-in-law, and never felt at home. She soon became pregnant, and in that condition had cravings for articles of delicacy, in which she did not dare indulge in my mother's presence. She would obtain and secrete bits of cake, preserves and other niceties, as she found opportunity, and would eat them in her own room or out of sight. After our boy was born and had become sufficiently grown to sit at the table, we noticed that while there he would never eat any piece of cake, pie, or other delicacy that was offered him, but if possible would secrete a piece and go away slyly in a corner or behind a door and greedily devour it there. At first we thought this only an amusing freak of childhood, and called it cunning; but after a time it became annoying. We wondered at it and tried to break it up, but without avail. He soon began to take other things, but we thought it only a common, childish fault, and hoped it would be outgrown. When he was but a few years old, I took him one day to a store to buy him a pair of shoes. His eye fell on a pair of boy's boots which took his fancy, and he said he wanted them. I thought shoes preferable, and purchased a pair. When we reached home I was pained to find that he had the boots hidden under his coat. I reprimanded him, reasoned with him and tried to show him the wickedness of the theft; but he insisted that he wanted the boots, and was going to have them. I told him he must take them back and

tell the storekeeper he was sorry ; but he stub-
bornly refused. I compelled him to go with me
and return the boots, but not a word of regret
could I induce him to utter. From that time on-
ward my troubles increased. In spite of all we
could say or do the boy would appropriate whatever he could lay his hands on that pleased his
fancy. All my property has been spent in paying
fines and rescuing him from the consequences of
his evil propensity ; the peace of my family has
been destroyed and 1 am a broken-hearted man
—all for the sake of saving a few paltry dollars at
the beginning of my married life ! Poor boy ! I
know he cannot help stealing, and therefore I am
glad he is where he can have no chance to steal."

The two following cases are from **Mrs. Pendleton:**

"Mrs. A—— was a melancholy instance of
strength of mind perverted to selfish ends. Am-
bitious of power and influence, she was unscrupulous in the means by which they were obtained.
Owing to her plausibility and pertinacity, she
once was elected to an office of trust in a benevo-
lent society of which she was a member. This
was a situation of great temptation to one whose
selfish sentiments predominated, as the event

proved ; for at the expiration of a year she was dismissed under the imputation of having appropriated a portion of the funds of the society to her own use. During the year in which she held this office, Mrs. A—— gave birth to a daughter, whose first characteristic manifestations were a marked tendency to theft."

An Unhappy Disposition.—The lovely Louisa M——, an intimate friend of the writer, remarkable for her good sense and kindness of disposition, at the age of twenty-five married a man of superior abilities, enjoying the advantages of an ample fortune and the best society. Their residence was charmingly situated, overlooking a noble river, great extent and variety of country, and surrounded by many beautiful objects of nature. The interior arrangements comprehended all that was desirable in the way of literature and the arts ; noted, also, as the abode of hospitality and the kindliest feelings. Thus situated, their children were born under the most happy influences—were beautiful, bright, and some of them highly talented. At the age of thirty-eight the mother ceased bearing children, and felt happy at the thought of being at length free from the confinement attending the cares of infancy. This state of things continued a few years, but was unexpectedly changed by symptoms of pregnancy. This was a most unwelcome prospect for one who had entered into the dissipation of fashionable life, and was determined in future to enjoy and not suffer. To avoid the approaching calamity, various means were resorted to, but were unsuccessful. After much discontent and repining, a girl was born, inheriting a large portion of the unhappy, repining and bitter temper which possessed the mother for months previous to her birth. The attempt to violate the laws of the Creator in this instance has been most signally punished, for in the perverse, rebellious spirit and cloudy brow of her unhappy daughter, the mother now recognizes the temper in which she so imprudently indulged during her pregnancy."

A Happy Disposition.—Dr. A. Newton gives the following case :

" In a certain family, well known to the writer, there are three children. The first two were undesired, and they exhibit various peculiar traits, such as were to have been expected from the conditions which preceded their birth. Among these are occasional fits of despondency and gloom, when for the time life seems to have no interest and the world no place for them, and they wonder why they were born. These are evidently but the reflex of the mother's moods at times during their gestation. The third was a welcome child. All the mother's energies were directed cheerfully and lovingly to its ante-natal fostering and culture. This child, now grown to young womanhood, is markedly different in temperament and general characteristics from either of the others. From her birth, she was a sunbeam of joy in the household, never causing a sleepless hour, even in infancy, by petulance or irritability, and never a shadow of grief to her parents' hearts. On the contrary, she has ever been a cheerful, dutiful, helpful and happy child, loving and beloved by all who know her within and without the family circle. She evidently feels that she has a right to be in the world, that it has a place for her, and has a disposition to do all in her power to make the world better and happier.

Ability and Amiability.—The two following cases occurred in my own experience. The first case is that of the bright, happy little girl of Mrs. M——, and is given in her own words as she wrote it out for me :

" When Mrs. M—— became pregnant, she determined to insure for her child a cheerful, happy disposition. Knowing something of pre-natal influence, and having a pretty strong will, she tried to prevent herself from ever being upset by anything.[1] She strove with all her might to keep happy and cheerful. She read books of a pleasant, interesting nature, and having a fondness for music, she indulged her taste extensively. So well did she succeed that not only is the child of a beautiful disposition, but also most talented, for she is naturally of a literary and musical bent of mind.''

A Bright, Sunny Disposition.—The second case is that of a child whose disposition is unequalled by that of any I have ever met with among the young or old. Although I knew the family well, I had never had much occasion to test the character of the children until in the autumn of 1890, when I was called to attend the two boys, who

---

* Many mothers while pregnant are inclined to be morbid, which condition, if not fought against, will most certainly affect the child. But this is never necessary, for no matter what the tendency to be morbid, selfish, etc., if only the mother will struggle against it, even if not altogether successful, the child will surely reap the benefit of her effort. This is why many women who have been in an unhappy state of mind during pregnancy, yet who fought against it, have had amiable children.

had scarlet fever of the most malignant type. I was in the house constantly during the day, and for ten nights, with the exception of a few hours, was there all the time. The difference in disposition of the two children was wonderful. The eldest boy, at that time eight years old, was quiet and even morose, while the younger was always bright and cheerful. It was so not only under ordinary circumstances, but under the most trying. Those who have had any experience with scarlet fever complicated with diphtheria know how extremely trying on the child is the attention that has to be given to the throat. Yet all the time that he was sick I never once knew him to complain, no matter what the ordeal he went through. Even at night, when he would have to be wakened up to have his throat attended to, he was cheerful, and would say with a smile, "Do you want to look at my throat, doctor?" On one occasion, when I remarked to his mother how unusual it was to see such a disposition in a child so young, she said, "S—— is always cheerful, no matter when I have had to wake him at night. He has always been good-natured; he is the sunshine of my life." She continued and gave me the following history:

When she was pregnant with her second child, six years previous to this time, an old friend whom she had not seen since they had been classmates, years before, paid her a visit, and a jolly time they had, as she expressed it. They went over the old times of their childhood days, and with this and the bright, witty stories and jokes of her friend, they were constantly in a state of merriment. The mother said, "Even when we were not together I used to laugh to myself over the stories R—— would tell." Thus is the history of this fortunate of fortunate children. I will further add that the mother was of an even disposition. The father was morose and sullen, while the eldest boy was of a quiet, retiring disposition, and, as his mother says, "a regular bookworm." It was purely a matter of accident that her child was so dispositioned, as the mother knew nothing of the power she had over her child while pregnant, although it is to this mighty influence and this alone that her child's happy disposition is due.

Would that all mothers could be so situated during the most critical period of their child's life! Even if she has to sacrifice other things—her pleasure as well—it is nothing more than what should be expected of her.   What are nine months of a little self-denial compared with years of tiresome toil with a fretful, peevish child ; and can a few months of the mother's life be compared to the lifelong happiness and success of her child, and that of future generations ?

Many more illustrations might be given, but it is not our desire to overload this volume.   Any reader need but observe the offspring of families in his immediate vicinity—observe the great difference in children of a near age, of the same parents, to obtain further evidence of the reality of pre-natal influence.

In the foregoing cases we have seen instances where parents entirely lacking in any special talent have had the most gifted children.   Nor was this due to education, for in nearly every instance this latent talent developed itself strongly in early life.   That the cultured and able-minded have children entirely wanting in their parents' good qualities, is a well-known fact.

There are cases where the children possessed beauty of face and form, the parents of whom were entirely devoid of it ; we have also seen that a child can be almost perfect in physique and constitution whose parents are far from being so.

We have seen instances where the most virtuous, refined parents have had the most depraved children, and we have seen those of happy disposition have the most unhappy children, as well as those not remarkable for their amiability have the most amiable, cheerful, sunny-natured children. To sum it up, we have seen instances in which physical, intellectual or moral characteristics have appeared in the offspring of parents who have been wanting entirely or to a great measure in such attributes, and that in every instance it has been due to pre-natal influence. Like two chords strung in unison, if we strike one the other vibrates ; so the fœtus responds to the maternal tension.

In concluding this chapter, with the facts before us, we find it necessary to draw only the two following conclusions :

First. Through pre-natal influence, we have the power to shape and mould the physical, mental and moral characteristics of our children.

Second. Every couple producing offspring are solemnly responsible to their Maker, to society and to future generations for the physical, intellectual and moral characteristics they impart to the offspring they bring forth.

When it is observed that a statistician has estimated that every couple producing offspring may calculate upon over four millions of descendants in five hundred years, what may not a mother do to bless or curse thousands of her descendants?

CHAPTER IV.

Requisites for Having a Well-Born Child.

" It is the right of every child to be well born."

IT is the right of every child to be well born, with a healthy body and a pure, healthy mind, with the seeds of only goodness and nobleness sown. Such children would be able to live healthy, happy and successful lives, and would be an unfailing source of pleasure to all around them. All parents desiring children must wish them to be such. The possibility to all for having such children has been demonstrated in the foregoing chapters. For we have seen the ignorant producing the talented and capable ; the cultured and virtuous producing the stupid and vicious. We have also seen that these results are produced during pregnancy, and, as already stated, some weeks prior to conception should also be included in the period of pre-natal influence.

Men of genius, as well as fools, are born and not made. But this does not mean that the parents of that genius or that fool had no power to alter his apparent destiny. Poets, artists and inventors, as well as all great men, are not made by education or training ; they are and must be born with the quality of genius, else all the teaching and training of a lifetime will be of no avail. That children of any class are born with as much or as little mental capacity as their parents, is eminently untrue. We seldom find that either the parents or children of great men have been remarkable for the genius which the one has apparently transmitted, and the other should have inherited.

If, then, the quality of the children can be predetermined by the parents, it is important to know those conditions which will produce the best offspring. Those essential conditions are, first, that the parents be well mated ; second, that they be in sound health ; third, that measures be taken to modify the evil qualities which exist in the parents ; fourth, that the parents secure for themselves the most favorable conditions during conception and pregnancy.

First. The parents should be mated so that the strong points of the one balance the weak points of the other, that the results may be a harmonious blending. This subject will be further dealt with in Part III., Chapter 3.

Second. The parents must be free from disease before allowing conception to take place. If either parent is suffering from any incurable disease, they should on no account propagate ; for no man has the right to bring into the world a sickly organism, to be handicapped during its existence, to be a detriment to the world, a burden to its friends, and to hand on its own infirmities and weaknesses. This is not meant to debar those who are simply delicate or suffering from mere functional trouble, but only those actually organically diseased. Fortunately there are few who cannot, if they will, have healthy children. "The natural law is that a weak and imperfectly organized frame transmits one of a similar description to offspring, and the children, inheriting weakness, are prone to fall into disease and die. Indeed, the transmission of various diseases founded in physical imperfections from parents to children is a matter of universal notoriety ; thus consumption, gout, scrofula, hydrocephalus, rheumatism and insanity are well known to descend from generation to generation. Strictly speaking, it is not *disease* which is transmitted, but organs of such imperfect structure that they are unable to perform their functions properly, and so weak that they are easily put into a morbid condition by causes which sound organs could easily resist.'"[1]

Third. It is important that the parents observe in themselves those good qualities which are weak and those bad qualities which are strong, that in transmitting them to the child the one may be intensified and the other diminished. For their *ruling tendencies*, modified by pre-natal circumstances, will certainly be transmitted, and the parents should take care that the qualities are to the child's advantage. Any evil tendencies or bad habits must not only be overcome, but *positively hated*, and this hatred of evil will be born in the child. Thus those of evil tendencies, whether it be inebriety or other vices, can, if they will, have children with sufficient force of character to resist the vices to which the parents were subject. Any who are not capable of such effort to overcome serious faults for love of their offspring, are unworthy to procreate them and should avoid their conception.

Fourth. The first three conditions having been complied with—that is, that the parents be well mated, in healthy condition and having overcome

---

[1] Combe's " Moral Philosophy."

their evil tendencies to the best of their ability— they should take advantage of pre-natal influence, which is the fourth requirement. This teaches that not only is the time during actual pregnancy of importance to the child, but also the moment of conception and *several weeks* prior to it, for what the parents are during these periods, that the child will be.

Not only must the parents' minds be upon what they wish their child to become, some weeks before conception, but they must also avoid the generative act for *at least* two weeks prior to that time, for the generation of the finest children. The creation of the new being must be *deliberate*, the time having been determined *beforehand*. There must be no chance, haphazard conception. For the child to get the best qualities of each parent, conception must occur when their vitality is the highest, which is in the morning, when the mind and body are refreshed from the fatigues of the preceding day. Furthermore, parental love must predominate and not mere sensual lust.

Under these circumstances, allowing that conception has taken place, a new being has been formed ; and now commences the most critical period in man's existence. This new being is much more susceptible to impressions than at any time after birth. Now is the time when untold, inestimable good may be done ; even supposing the circumstances of conception and those prior to it have *not* been the most favorable, a vast deal can yet be accomplished. No aim for its future can be too high, for nearly everything within the possibilities of human attainment can be secured.

From this time until birth the developing child is most susceptible to influence through the mother, as the illustrations given in the preceding chapter have demonstrated. In this tender, delicate state, the mind and body are just forming ; that which will govern the child's whole future life is developing. The child can be moulded into almost any state of mind and body. The true mother will be ever mindful of her most sacred trust, and will surround herself with circumstances which will conduce to the *perfect development* of the child in *body and mind.*

The direction in which these efforts should be made will be outlined below. More detailed directions as to diet, bathing, exercise, dress, etc., will be found in the chapter on " Hygiene of Pregnancy."

Physical and Physiological Development.

Strength and Activity.—In order to obtain these qualities in the child, the mother must *daily* direct her power to every part of her muscular system —that is, that she make use of light gymnastics, exercising the *arms*, the *back* and the *legs*. Be the exercise ever so little, it must be a daily practice. On the other hand, she should guard against working beyond her strength either at exercise or manual labor, in which case the child would probably lack vigor.

Breathing or Lung Power.—In either physical or mental labor the quality of *endurance* is largely dependent upon the depth and activity of the lungs. One of the greatest blessings a woman can impart to her child is capacity for work. She may confer genius upon it, but if she does not give it the physical force to develop and sustain this latent ability, the former is of little value. Therefore by all means every woman should transmit to her child good lung power ; and this she can do by a careful course of breathing exercises.

Strong Blood Circulation.—With persistent gymnastics and breathing exercises, each of which should be commenced very carefully and gently, gradually increasing in time and vigor, the heart will gain power, and a strong circulation will be developed in both mother and child.

Digestive and Assimilative Power.—Second only to lung power is the ability to take in all kinds of food and convert it into blood, which nourishes and strengthens the body and the brain. This power, as with the others, is transmitted by the mother by caring for her corresponding organs. Her selection of food should be simple and nourishing, discarding sweets, pastry and rich food, condiments, tea and coffee ; especially should she avoid *overloading* the stomach. However, she must be supplied with food which she relishes, but she must not let her mind dwell too much on eating or drinking, that the child may not thereby be made a glutton. Breakfast should be the principal meal ; the evening meal should always be light and the utmost regularity should be observed as to the meal hour. Furthermore, the bowels should be kept regular, as their inaction is related to many disorders of the bodily functions.

A Good Constitution.—A good constitution is one in which the foregoing organs and functions are strong. The mother who transmits each of these essentials imparts to her offspring a vitality which is strong to resist disease and is quick to recover : which makes living a pleasure and life a success.

The mother has already gathered from the Cases, the manner in which beauty of face and symmetry of form have been imparted (pp. 78–88) ; of these methods she can easily take advantage.

Mental and Moral Development.

Social Faculties.—The mother wishes her child to enjoy friendships, to be capable of attracting and holding friends. Some children are shy and self-distrustful ; they see the friendships of others, but do not understand them nor the steps necessary to make a friend. Misunderstood, they work out their unhappy lives in loneliness, which might have been brightened by friendly intercourse. To avoid this in her child, then, she should not shut herself away from her friends, but freely enjoy their society and companionship.

She would have them fond of their home and of their parents ; she would have them remember home incidents with pleasure, for as a man is ruled by his passions, so does his fondness for the home people often protect him from the baser forms of affection. By interesting herself in her home surroundings—the furniture, the pictures, the household pets—by picturing to herself her child's life and growth among these, her possessions, she will implant in it the impulses which she desires.

The little stranger should be *welcome* to the nest she is providing for it. It should be impressed with those pleasant feelings with which we anticipate what is agreeable. There is a superstition among the Irish that those children who are received as blessings from God prove to be so, and that those who are not received as such turn out the contrary. It is certainly true that children who have, during pregnancy, been regarded as nuisances or necessary evils are often of a warped or disappointing disposition.

Therefore, mothers, welcome your child ; fill it with instincts of affection and confidence. In its future life you will have little control over its love or its wilfulness. " What shall we do with our wayward child ?" write the mothers to the " Home" column of the journals. " Make a friend of your child," is the invariable answer.

Many a mother has tried this prescription, and has known the heartache and the sorrow when she finally realized that her child's heart had gone from her and was fixed on other idols, that it needed no friendship of hers and desired none. Therefore we say, love your unborn child *now*, for now you can fix upon it the love which, in the days when your power exists no longer, will hold that child true to you for life.

Among the social faculties, the most powerful is that which attracts the sexes. So strongly does this sense appeal to the modern man, that he sacrifices his good name, his self-respect, risks all disease and danger to gratify his passion. Moralists have condemned him, physicians have warned, reformers have exhorted him and laws have been enacted for years, but this sensual passion, in the majority of men and many women of to-day, is virtually uncontrollable. The many methods which have been tried in the effort to check or at least regulate this evil have thus far been failures. That heredity refuses to transmit the virtues of the parents is a notable fact; but this does not prove that the vice is unconquerable; it merely shows that the present methods of dealing with it are insufficient. In pre-natal influence we have an instrument of tremendous power ; it is capable of dealing effectually with this moral pestilence.. As the mother, then, values the purity of her sons and the chastity of her daughters, she will keep her thoughts pure and her imaginings controlled. She need not stifle her love for her husband. On the contrary, she should love him and trust him the more dearly ; but caresses must be controlled, they must not be permitted to arouse strong personal feelings ; their thoughts should be rather upon their child than upon each other, and, above all, the generative act should be avoided. To this end husband and wife should occupy separate rooms, or at least separate beds ; should they fail, however, in their efforts to control their passions entirely, they should not yield oftener than once, or at most twice, a month.

Practical Faculties.—The practical mental powers are important. They are those which give man his energy and his determination in taking care of his material welfare. In her gymnastic exercising the mother will develop qualities of strength and endurance. If she persist in these simple, hygiene practices which are most often neglected, she will endow the child.with that quality of *perseverance* which most often achieves success.

The good housekeeper is of economical mould ; she knows how to utilize the little bits, to turn everything to account, like the French cooks. If naturally lacking in this quality, the mother should cultivate it by force of will, curbing extravagant tastes, and trying to realize, if she has not already done so, the labor and the toil which one dollar represents. And she should do this not with motives of personal household economy in mind, but that her child may not develop into a reckless spendthrift, which is too often the case with those born of wealthy parents. If this quality alone were transmitted, the child would be covetous and miserly. It must be balanced by a *generosity*, a spending of money and time not on one's self, but upon others. Man was not meant to be a miser, neither to be a careless giver, unthinking of his own needs and the needs of those dependent upon him. Both qualities should be possessed in equal degree ; then in his giving and his saving the intellect is free to decide and act unhampered by ruling impulses.

Any attempt on the part of the mother to destroy her child before birth is liable, if unsuccessful, to result in producing *murderous tendencies.* Even harboring murderous thoughts, whether toward her own child or not, might be followed by similar results. Guiteau was a marked example of this, whose case will be found in Part II., Chapter I.

While the destructive quality is important to possess in some degree, as it gives the power of doing things *thoroughly and quickly*, the mother should guard against overdeveloping it. With this faculty should be developed the quality of *perseverance*. Whatever the mother undertakes she should follow to the end, not lagging or postponing in her self-imposed tasks.

This brings us to the subject of *anger*, fits of *passion* and *rebellion* against one's station in life. If the mother but realized how each passionate outbreak stamped its stimulus upon the germ within, if she could but foresee her tempestuous nature perpetuated in her child, the anger which she has dispersed upon those around her rebounding upon her from that child in after life, she would make a strong effort to bind down her too irascible spirit.

Transmitting of *thieving and sneaking* tendencies and of *untruthfulness* can easily be avoided. Any one versant with human nature understands the value of this precaution. A perusal of the cases, pp. 88–102, will indicate the steps which are necessary for this. The mother's life should be honest, fearless and confident.

Inordinate opinion of one's own ability or person, coupled with extreme sensitiveness to the opinion of others, keeps many people in mental misery. *Pride* and *conceit*, if present, are apt to be permanent faults of the mother. They should have been overcome in both parents before the time of conception, in obedience to the third requirement for a well-born child. But sensitiveness, bashfulness, self-consciousness, may be easily developed by pre-natal circumstances. The mother may protect her child from these by overcoming her natural sensitiveness to her delicate condition, and by turning pride of birth or beauty into pride of motherhood.

Fright, anxiety and care should not be allowed to mould the growing mind, and from these the expectant father must protect his wife.

Cheerfulness must predominate. "When there is no hope there can be no endeavor," said Samuel Johnson. Hope is an excellent quality for a human being to possess. It saves him from many a worry, and softens many a discomfort with its kindly touch. In fact, *hope, faith and charity* are the basis of all true morality—hope for the future, present faith in the goodness of God's purposes, and a charity which receives and sympathizes with all men. Endow your child with these attributes, and you give him a religion and a philosophy which will serve him the world around.

Mothers have only to give way to a dislike and disgust for *religion* to have the most irreligious children. Therefore respect things sacred. Conscientious acceptance of the responsibilities and performance of the duties of child-bearing will suffice to implant in the child *conscientiousness*.

One great cause of trouble in the rearing of a family is the constantly fretful, irritable, peevish dispositions of the children, entailing on the parents a world of trouble in their care and management. Now, it is just as easy that a mother should secure for her child a cheerful, sunny nature, that will be to her in truth and in deed "the sunshine of life," as it is to give birth to a child of a fretful and unhappy disposition, which is to her a source of lifelong trouble. To this end the parents should not permit themselves to be worried over the petty trials of the day. They should take the accidents of life good-naturedly, and endeavor "to laugh dull care away."

There is a class of faculties which, while not directly supporting the material life, contribute to making that life pleasurable and refined. These are the perceptive ideas of beautiful forms, of grand creations, either of earth or in ideas. The painter's brush, the sculptor's chisel, the poet's pen, are surrounding us with food for these desires. They are *refining* influences, and should be brought to bear upon the child.

Intellectual Faculties.—"I add this also, that natural ability without education has oftener raised man to glory and virtue, than education without natural ability."—*Cicero.*

The *desire for knowledge* is the first requirement in education ; the *capacity for knowledge* is the second. Such is the operation of the pre-natal law, that desire and effort on the part of the mother becomes desire and capacity in the child. The mother must apply herself to learning, and in the direction in which the strongest effort is made will be the child's development.

There are, however, certain qualities which every child should possess, irrespective of his special purposes, and these the mother must cultivate in herself. First is power of *application.* With the ability to apply one's self solely to the subject in hand, learning is an easy matter.   It is the child who cannot apply himself, whose attention is distracted by every butterfly passing the window or the car-bells on the street, to whom the acquirement of book learning is difficult.

Another important faculty is that of *memory*— of events, of words, of faces and of numbers. Let the mother read history, memorize dates of noted events, recall to her mind the happenings of yesterday or of last week, memorize poetry or speeches, try to recall faces and numbers from her past experiences.

Reasoning power, ability to discriminate between that which is logically right and that which is logically wrong, *precision* in study, which does not allow of careless, slovenly reading, but insists that a fact be remembered correctly, that an incident be strictly reported according to the facts— these should be possessed by every human mind. An attempt to study higher mathematics, geometry and algebra is the best way of influencing the child.   If, however, she is averse to these studies, let her study sermons and speeches ; ask herself if they are true, and why, and if the point has been proven.

Acquirement of knowledge should not be confined merely to books. The mother should train the eye to judge *distances, heights and weights;* and the mind to calculate *figures.*

Habits of *system, order and method* should be especially cultivated. *Order* is the first great law of nature. Order of thought, of mind, of person, of surroundings, of action, is essential to success in all departments of life. Great workers are *systematic* workers. Such men as Gladstone, Napoleon, and those who have become eminent in political, commercial and professional life, not only had the genius for their work, but they were systematic in applying it. They had "a time for everything" and "everything in its place." Appreciation of times and hours should be cultivated by the mother arranging her work, her rest hour, her meals at definite hours, and keeping them *precisely.* In all the parents do, from the least thing to the greatest, they should carefully observe *order and punctuality,* and especially should these be cultivated if they are deficient in either parent.

We do not expect that with one reading of the foregoing scheme the mother will become familiar with all that is required of her; she must constantly refer to it. Many of the desired qualities she may already have. These it is not necessary for her to develop, unless there be some qualities which are overactive and must be restrained. Let her study her own nature, make good in her child what is deficient in herself and her husband, and restrain those qualities which they possess too strongly. We do not expect that she will become a paragon of virtue and intellect. We simply ask her to make an *honest, earnest effort*, such an effort which is *possible to every human being*, an effort to fit her child for a *strong, honorable, and successful career*.

Special Talent.—"Genius must be born, and never can be taught."—*Dryden.*

If the mother follows the suggestions already given, she will produce " a well-born child." It is well, though, that every child should be imbued with some *special talent*, which, if developed, will enable it to pursue a definite calling. What this talent shall be is in the mother's power to choose. The parents should determine before conception what they wish their child to be ; and whether it be an artist or a mechanic, they should centre their minds upon this individual thing for at least a month prior to that time, and during pregnancy the mother should continue this concentration. They should study the subject of art or mechanics, throw their whole energy into it, talk about it, think about it. If they have chosen for their child a calling upon which they can enter, such as literature, music, painting, modelling, oratory, or mechanical drawing, let them engage in it and throw their whole minds into it. In this way they can have at will literary men, musicians, artists, sculptors, orators, mechanics, engineers, architects, business men, doc· tors, lawyers, theologians, etc.

It must be clearly borne in mind that in order to impart these attributes, the parents need not *learn* the desired trade or profession, but we do require that they try to learn it. Try hard, try persistently, try constantly during the period of pre-natal influence, and the results will more than exceed your greatest hopes and desires. Remember that the child is susceptible to this influence at *any time during pregnancy.* No matter how good the physique or what the mental attainments of the parents prior to conception, if they do not regard the foregoing requirements the child may be ruined by the mother's mode of living during pregnancy, as by her diet, dress and surroundings. If she live a life of idle, selfish enjoyment of any kind, her child will probably reap the results in being an idle, dissipated, selfish man or woman. If she is constantly brooding over trouble, either real or imaginary, more or less low-spirited and melancholy, her child will probably be timid and shrinking, with no vim or energy, always melancholy, and might possibly end in an asylum or fill a suicide's grave. The mother *must not worry* over the result, must not distrust her own efforts, for this anxiety will be transmitted to the child; she must cultivate a bright, cheerful disposition, and be ever mindful that hers is the *most sacred and honorable state*. Let her recognize the importance of her situation, and be proud of her high and noble condition. Would that the ancient custom now prevailed which required from all due reverence being shown to one in that hallowed state.

Father's Duty.—"He who is false to present duty breaks a thread in the loom, and will find the flaw when he may have forgotten its cause." —*Henry Ward Beecher.*

Hitherto we have pointed out principally the duties of the mother, but it must not be supposed that the father's duties end with the time of conception. He has yet to play a part which is second to none other. He must be in *perfect accord* with the purposes and aspirations of the expectant mother. Her plans should be his plans, her hopes his hopes. He will do his utmost to assist her in *retaining good health ;* to see that she is *happy and contented,* free from *excessive work, and guarded from care and trouble.* He will do all in his power to give her every intellectual opportunity. She must have recourse to literature, art, music and intellectual friends. He must remember that she is forming *his* child. He will *bear* with her in all *trying circumstances.* He will *avoid* arousing her passions and his own, for he must not pollute his child's mind by indulging during pregnancy. Furthermore, he will do everything conducive to her comfort and welfare and that of his child's. He who is truly *deserving* of the name of husband and father will carry out these duties to the *fullest* extent of his ability.

In concluding this chapter, we cannot do better than quote the words of that distinguished physician and thinker, Dr. Selden H. Talcott, Superintendent of one of the New York State Hospitals for the Insane :

' In all begetting there is either an increasing or a decreasing intensity of likeness. In all reproduction there is a tendency either toward improvement or toward retrogression. This is true not only as regards physical contour, but it also applies to mental symmetry or mental idiosyncrasy. Not only are the general thoughts and emotions of the parents impressed upon their children, but even the flitting passion of a moment · may cast a cloud of darkness or a blaze of light over an entire life, just as the silvered sheet of the photographer receives its impressions of light and shade from a single momentary exposure. The mind of the unborn child will receive impressions of happy or unholy thoughts, and reproduce them with accuracy in the years to come—aye, even when the brain of the mother is but dust and her heart no longer responds to any emotion, and her guiding hand has been chilled by the icy touch of death. To this holy of holies, then, the sacred temple of procreation, should be brought only such offerings as are sure to prove acceptable to the Lord of Nature.

" Bright surroundings, pleasant associations, stimulating encouragement, abundant food of the best quality and of the most easily assimilated kind, air, exercise and sunlight, together with simple direction, not forcing of the mental faculties, will, in course of patient time, produce from even poor stock such a robust and cultured race as to be the astonishment of those who furnish and mould the material.''

CHAPTER V.

Conclusion.

" Every mission constitutes a pledge of duty. Every man is bound to consecrate his every faculty to its fulfilment. He will derive his rule of action from the profound conviction of that duty." —MAZZINI.

MAN is nature's greatest work. In his intricate organization, which gives him almost unlimited power, is he truly wonderful. He is far above the lower animals, with complete control and mastery over them ; and yet how much more interest is taken in breeding fine stock than in having fine children !

Stock-raisers take every possible precaution in breeding to obtain only the best results. They will tell you stock-raising is a science, and one that requires careful study and discrimination ; that race-horses are *born, not made.* In mating horses to get the best results, they are most careful not only as to the breed of the sire and dam, but also that the temperament, disposition and form will harmonize. This is not all ; during the whole time, the expected mother has the greatest care taken of her ; her surroundings are the most favorable ; and it would be considered outrageous to think of allowing the male to approach her. The fine horses of the present day and fine stock of every class are the result only of such breeding.

On all sides we hear discussed the latest devices for the improvement of stock, and yet almost nothing is said or thought as to the improvement of our own offspring. The subject seems to be lacking in interest and enthusiasm on all sides. The human race is thrown together in one conglomerate mass, to mate with any one and every one, regardless of health, temperament, disposition, relationship or position. Two thirds of the unions are not love matches, and not one match in ten thousand is made with the definite idea of living natural, healthy lives and producing natural, healthy offspring. This applies to all classes, rich or poor, high or low. What can be expected, then, of the children from such unions? They were conceived in a haphazard way, born when not wanted, of parents who had no control of their passions in any sense of the word, and with surroundings far from favorable.

From generation to generation bad habits, vice and weakness are transmitted with hardly an effort made to rectify them. Is it any wonder, then, that the vast number of sufferers, ne'er-do-weels, imbeciles, and criminals is swelled to a more and more alarming extent? Is it any wonder that half of the human race perish under ten years of age?

Nor is this all. Because a child is not sound in body and mind is not to say it will not mature or attain the allotted period of man's existence--not at all; for on all sides, in nearly every family, there are plain instances of this—individuals who go through life with hardly a well day; others who suffer very little, and between the two every degree of disease, misery and misfortune, all more or less handicapped, and why? Simply because of ignorance on the parents' part; for it cannot be that they would be guilty of so outrageous a crime as to *knowingly* bring into the world unhealthy, impure, but innocent babes, only to fill early graves, or swell the now overflowing stream of those whose lives are a failure, physically, mentally and morally.

Because man is naturally imperfect, and will always be so, is not to say that evil should predominate and not good; and it is only in such cases with badly balanced minds that checks in the way of punishment and confinement are needed.

All institutions for confinement or punishment, with a view to improvement of the human race ; all societies, religious organizations, as well as every popular work done for the betterment of mankind, are only dealing with the effect, not the cause. Their work never will be ended as long as they do not go back to the root of the evil and endeavor to launch human beings on the sea of life with healthy bodies and pure, healthy minds. Then only can permanent improvement be looked for from any effort made to better the race.

Thousands of human souls are born into the world every day, and of these the majority go to swell the crowded ranks of the unfortunate and imperfect class, whether unfortunate in their career or imperfect in mind or body—many so weak-minded, so naturally vicious and incapable of deriving benefit from what is good that they are beyond the reach of man.

It is to prevent these unfortunates from being so born that efforts must be made for the welfare of the race by all agencies at command, to have them sound in body and mind, free from contamination of disease and vice, capable of unlimited attainment. That this is within the power of all well-meaning people at all capable of having children is beyond doubt.

And now that it is known how to have such children, let the aim be to have them. Let no woman shirk the sacred functions of motherhood. Why should she? Are not children the greatest blessing, the greatest source of happiness bestowed on mankind?

Child-bearing, under favorable circumstances, improves the health. Many a delicate, frail woman has bloomed into a robust, healthy mother.

Children are part of their parents—something to live for; something that will live after them, to enjoy what they have left, to perpetuate the race and maintain the family name. Truly has Longfellow said:

> "What would the world be to us,
> If the children were no more!"

In no way can the parents better show to the world what they are than by their children. They come next our hearts, are something we can love and cherish, and who will return it in old age. They are a bond of union between

mother and father, often keeping them from drift-
ing apart. They help us to be unselfish, they
sweeten and soften our natures, and teach us lessons which only children can teach.

> " They are idols of hearts and of households,
>   They are angels of God in disguise."

This subject gives every one an aim in life ;
for whether or not it is in their power to have
well-born children, it is their duty to impart to
others what they know. It is a duty and yet a
pleasure, for true happiness is only obtained by
making others happy. This is charity, and charity is love, and love is the greatest of all things.
It is to love we owe our existence ; it is by love
our way was bought to heaven ; it is love that
makes us bear and forbear ; it is the strongest
part of character. Truly love is the truest,
purest, strongest, noblest thing in all the world !

" Miserable it is
To be to others cause of misery,
Our own begotten, and of our loins to bring
Into this cursed world a woful race ;
.   .   .   .   .   in thy power
It lies, yet ere conception to prevent
The race unblessed, the being yet unbegot."

—MILTON's *Paradise Lost,* Book X.

PART II.

LIMITATION OF OFFSPRING.

Introduction.

"Chance, though blind, is the sole author of the creation."
—J. X. B. SAINTINE.

IN Part I. we have given the essentials for a well-born child, and have shown how such children may be secured by nearly all well-meaning parents. In order, however, for this to be accomplished, the parents must be able to choose a time when they are in their best physical, mental and moral state to conceive, and in a fit financial position to give both mother and child the required care. If parents cannot have this power of selection, they cannot have well-born children. For there must be a deliberate, not a chance, haphazard conception ; procreation, to yield the best results, *must be controlled.*

This control is accomplished in one of three ways : by chastity, abortion, or the prevention of conception. Abortion will be dealt with in the first chapter ; chastity and the prevention of conception in the second ; while the third chapter will be devoted to the means best adapted for this latter purpose.

CHAPTER I.

Abortion or Miscarriage.

" The great King of kings
Hath in the table of his law commanded,
That thou shalt do no murder : wilt thou then
Spurn at his edict, and fulfil a man's?
Take heed ; for he holds vengeance in his hand
To hurl upon their heads that break his law."
—RICHARD III., ACT I.

IN conception, the male sperm comes in contact with and impregnates the female ovum, or egg. If this impregnation occurs, a new being is formed and started on its longer or shorter existence. The taking of any measures to destroy this new life, to check its development or to remove it before its full term of preparation, is abortion, or miscarriage.

Sometimes, but rarely, it is necessary for a physician to bring on an abortion—that is, when, either from disease or deformity, the mother's life is unquestionably in danger should the pregnancy be allowed to continue. This is merely choosing the least of two evils, for abortion, no matter how skilfully performed, is dangerous to the mother's life at the time of operation, and paves the way for suffering and disease in her after life. Therefore it is a step which physicians undertake only after serious forethought, and only in an extreme case.

Occasionally miscarriage is produced accidentally by a fall or blow, and these cases are also very serious.

With these occasional exceptions, abortion is a twofold crime—a crime against morals and against health.

It is a *legal* or *moral crime* because it takes the life of a being which has a legal right to live. Many a woman who would shudder at the idea of strangling her nursing infant, has no compunctions in attempting abortion. Few outside of the medical profession have any idea of the alarming extent of this practice. All doctors who make women's diseases a specialty are repeatedly asked to perpetrate this felony. A woman will go to almost any extreme to rid herself of her unborn child, and many unscrupulous so-called doctors take advantage of her predicament to gratify their mercenary instincts. Besides these men of the regular profession, there are many unprinci-

pled scoundrels of both sexes who make a business of tempting women with their attractive
promises of safe and speedy relief. The crime of
abortion is rife to an appalling extent, and woman's conscience has become dulled by familiarity
with it.

Many a woman becomes pregnant, even when
bearing a child means disgrace to herself and
family ; or when her husband may not be able to
support another child ; or even though she may
be terrorized by the prospect of the agony of
childbirth. The inducements for abortion are
strong, and her weak human nature cannot always
resist. But how much better it would be if, in
these cases, conception had been prevented, as
surely would have been the case had the mother
understood the methods of prevention !

Were the masses of the people possessed of this
knowledge, it would save much sin and suffering
among them ; and in these days, when the courts
of our land cannot keep pace with the crimes of
its people, some more effective measure for reducing crime is strongly needed.

Abortion is a *physiological crime* because it is
ruinous to the mother's health. Even if the woman escapes death from blood-poisoning or peritoni-

tis shortly after the operation, the effects of this interference with the body processes are serious and long-lasting.

Led by the glittering advertisements and promises of unscrupulous quacks, women have come to believe that abortion is a simple and harmless process, while throughout all ages the pangs of childbirth have been cited as the acme of suffering. The fact is, that abortion is accompanied with far more danger and unhappy results than natural delivery.

The numerous intimate, complicated, sympathetic relations of the womb, or uterus, to every organ or part, near or distant, is most marvellous. The womb is the great centre upon which every other organ depends for its well-being, and is the great essential for woman's existence, health and happiness. When the uterus—this centre, this core of woman, around which she is built—is tampered with and outrageously devastated of that for which nature intended its existence, what wonder that it should become weakened and diseased, and her whole being thrown into a state of disorder! From abortion comes the danger of dreaded, deplorable disorders of the womb, or of almost any other organ of the body, with the train of general ill health following after. While these troubles may be temporary, they are liable to be present during the rest of the hapless victim's existence, and may not unlikely precipitate death.

While the mother's health and happiness are at stake, that of the child's is far more so should her attempts at fœticide be unsuccessful; for, as **Dr. Holbrook** says, "Some of the most wayward persons I have ever known were born of mothers who tried unsuccessfully to destroy them before birth. One was the child of a mother who did not know she was pregnant; her physician did not suspect it, and her efforts to bring on menstruation continued till the period of quickening, at which time the mistake was discovered, but quite too late to rectify the injury. This child, now a woman, is one of the most disagreeable characters, has no kindly feeling for her parents, is in no way equal to either of them physically, intellectually or morally. Such additions to the world's population are not desirable. They cost more to rear, they give more pain and trial, and return little pleasure to their parents and friends."

Guiteau.—Another still more deplorable case is that of Guiteau, the assassin of President Garfield.

It illustrates well the evils of attempting to produce abortion. His father was a man of considerable intellectual ability, of integrity of character, though there was evidently an insane
neurosis in the family. His children were born
in quick succession ; and the mother, who was in
poor health, was obliged to work harder than she
ought to do for lack of means to procure compe-
tent help. Before this child was born, she resorted to every means in her power, though unsuccessfully, to produce abortion, and for several
weeks during the latter part of pregnancy had
brain-fever, which probably caused an arrest of
development of some part of his brain. When the
child at last came into the world it was weak and
puny, and for many months its life was one continual wail. Months elapsed before its nervous
system became at all quiet.

Guiteau's whole life was full of contradictions.
There was little self-controlling power in him, no
common-sense, and not a vestige of remorse or
shame. In his imagination he believed himself
capable of doing the greatest work with no means,
and of filling the loftiest stations in life. It is
not to be doubted that his mother's efforts to
destroy him while in embryo and her illness had

much to do with bringing him to the level of the brutes.

Let no woman be guilty of this crime, for motherhood is the crowning of a woman's existence. Motherhood means, as a rule, health and life, and a new world of unlimited happiness and power for doing good ; while abortion, besides its enormity, means the dethronement of health and happiness —it is un-Christian, unjust, unprincipled, unnatural and unwomanly.

CHAPTER II.

Chastity and Prevention of Conception.

" To know
That which before us lies in daily life
Is the prime wisdom."
—MILTON.

WE now come to the consideration of the two remaining methods of controlling procreation—chastity and the prevention of conception. Chastity is the ideal procedure. It would also be the real one were all men and women

" Chaste as the icicle,
That's curded by the frost from purest snow
And hangs on Dian's temple."

Unfortunately this is not the case. Most men are born with inordinate sexual passion, and few are endowed with the power of controlling it. Therefore we must have some means more practicable than chastity, without the criminality and danger of abortion, and this we find in the prevention of conception.

It is to be hoped that in future generations virtue and purity will be so innate that the first-mentioned state will be generally possible. However, as men are at present constituted, no matter what their condition, they *will* have intercourse, and the natural consequence of intercourse is the birth of children. This occurrence in itself would be innocent enough were this the end of the matter ; but, on the contrary, this is only the beginning, for these children must be fed and educated, and must finally take on the responsibilities of manhood and womanhood whether they are fit for it or not.

We will quote from many writers eminent in scientific and philosophical studies, who trace the origin of much human misery and crime to this thoughtless, indiscriminate bringing of children into the world.

There are times and conditions when the birth of children is a wrong to the community. It is a wrong, either knowingly or ignorantly, to bring into the world, through no fault of its own, a being impure, unhealthy, and incomplete, only to suffer and die, or to live a life of misery and imperfection and perpetuate the curse in succeeding generations. Yet so much is this fact disregarded that one half the human race perish in early childhood.

Nor can this be wondered at when it is considered from what unsound seed they come and under what unfavorable circumstances many of them are conceived, born and reared. If people will violate nature's laws and have children by haphazard conception, when they are neither in a fit state of mind or body ; if they will continue to exert no favorable influence during gestation ; and if they will disregard all laws of health and reason in bringing up their children, then nature is only doing a kindness in keeping the world from ruination by wiping such misbegotten, unfortunate beings off the earth.

Is such a lesson sufficient to teach people their folly ? In some cases it is, but very often it is in vain, for, as **Mrs. Pendleton** says :

" Even when they have tasted the bitter consequence of their folly, they are far from recognizing the cause of their sufferings. With much self-complacency they resign themselves to the events, and seek consolation in religion. ' The Lord giveth,' say they, ' and the Lord taketh away ; blessed be the name of the Lord ! ' As if the Lord did not give men understanding, and impose on

them the obligation of using it to discover His
laws and obey them ; and as if there were no im-
piety in shutting their eyes against His laws, in
pretending to dispense with them ; and, finally,
when they are undergoing the punishment of
such transgressions, in appealing to Him for consolation."

Rev. M. J. Savage, in a sermon, reported in the
Boston *Transcript*, in 1876, declared :

" Some means ought to be provided for check-
ing the birth of sickly children."

Dr. Stockham writes in the same strain :

" Thoughtful minds must acknowledge the
great wrong done when children are begotten
under adverse conditions. Women must learn
the laws of life so as to protect themselves, and
not be the means of bringing sin-cursed, diseased
children into the world. *The remedy is in the prevention of pregnancy, not in producing abortion.*"

Pye H. Chavasse, F.R.C.S., etc., in his book
" Advice to a Wife," says :

" Feeble parents have generally feeble children ;
diseased parents, diseased children ; nervous parents, nervous children—' like begets like.' It is
sad to reflect that the innocent have to suffer not
only for the guilty, but for the thoughtless and

the inconsiderate.   Disease and debility are thus propagated from one generation to another, and the race becomes wofully deteriorated.   The above is a gloomy picture, and demands the efforts of all who love their country to brighten its sombre coloring. . . . Not only do children inherit the physical diseases, but they inherit likewise the moral and mental infirmities of their parents."

Professor Mantegazza, the distinguished Italian senator and anthropologist, says in his " Elements of Hygiene" :

" Hygiene has the most sacred right to say, in the name of science, to the tuberculous, the epileptic, the insane, the idiotic, the syphilitic, ' *Love, but do not have offspring.*'   And political economy, which is merely a hygiene of society, ought to say to the poor man who has nothing to offer his children but want or the foundling hospital, ' *Love, but do not have offspring.*' "

Even if the parents have good intentions and the circumstances are favorable, is it right to have so many children that they cannot be properly fed, clothed and educated ?   Besides the great injustice to the children themselves, they often become a burden to the State as criminals or paupers.

The **Earl of Pembroke** wrote to the *Pall Mall Gazette :*

"I am one of those who hold the doctrine, much misliked by the weaker sort of philanthropists, that both the poverty and the overcrowding, that are such a blot on our civilization, are mainly due to the continual and over-rapid increase of the population in the wage-earning class."

T. D. Nicholls, M.D., F.A.S., in "Esoteric Anthropology," p. 113, says :

"In the present social state, men and women should refrain from having children unless they see a reasonable prospect of giving them suitable nurture and education."

Montague Cookson, Q.C., in the *Fortnightly Review* for October, 1872, gives his opinion that

"The limitation of the number of the family . . . is as much the duty of married persons as the observance of chastity is the duty of those that are unmarried."

That renowned scientist, **Professor Huxley,** wrote, in the *Nineteenth Century* for February, 1888 :

"Let us be under no illusions, then. So long as unlimited multiplication goes on, no social organization which has ever been devised, or is likely to be devised, no fiddle-faddling with the distribution of wealth, will deliver society from the tendency to be destroyed by the reproduction within itself, in its intensest form, of that struggle for existence the limitation of which is the object of society."

John Stuart Mill, the great authority on logic and political economy, wrote :

" Every one has a right to live. We will suppose this granted. But no one has a right to bring children into life to be supported by other people. Whoever means to stand upon the first of these rights must renounce all pretension to the last." Again he says : " Little improvement can be expected in morality until the production of a large family is regarded in the same light as drunkenness or any other physical excess." [1]

Cotter Morison, in " The Service of Man," predicted :

" The criminality of producing children whom one has no reasonable probability of being able to keep, must in time be seen in its true light, as one of the most unsocial and selfish proceedings of which a man nowadays is capable. . . . If only

---

[1] " Principles of Political Economy."

the aevastating torrent of children could be arrested for a few years it would bring untold relief.''

Rev. H. R. Haweis, M.A., writing in the *Weekly Times and Echo,* November, 1886, declared :

'' Until it is thought a disgrace in every rank of society, from top to bottom of the social scale, to bring into the world more children than you are able to provide for, the poor man's home, at least, must often be a purgatory—his children dinnerless, his wife a beggar—himself too often drunk. . . . Here, then, are the real remedies : first, control the family growth according to the family means of support.''

Lester F. Ward states :

'' Artificial selection, now a settled principle in biology, must be applicable in its length and breadth to the human race. . . . If the opinion could prevail among all classes that the human race could be rapidly improved, both physically and mentally, by the intelligent selection of those who are to keep up the population, much of the difficulty would remove itself. If there is one social phenomenon which human *ingenuity* ought to bring completely under the control of the will, it is the phenomenon of procreation. Just as every one is his own judge of how much he shall eat and drink, of what commodities he wants to make life enjoyable, so every one should be his own judge of how large a family he desires, and should have power in the same degree to leave off when the requisite number is reached. What society needs is restriction of population, especially among the classes and at the points where it now increases most rapidly." [1]

Sismondi says :

" When dangerous prejudices have not become accredited, when our true duties toward those to whom we give life are not obscured in the name of a sacred authority, no married man will have more children than he can afford to bring up properly."

Mrs. Fawcett, who has studied pauperism and crime with a critical eye, thinks that

" Nothing will permanently offset pauperism while the present reckless increase of population continues ;" and **Rev. Leonard Dawson,** in a lecture reported in the *Alnwick and County Gazette*, February 11th, 1888, said :

" How rapidly conjugal prudence might lift a

Dynamic Sociology," vol. ii., pp. 463–66.

nation out of pauperism was seen in France. . . .
Let them therefore hold the maxim that the production of offspring with forethought and providence is rational nature. It was immoral to
bring children into the world whom they could
not reasonably hope to feed, clothe and educate. . . . Let them rest assured that he considered his views truly Christian, and likely to pro-
mote the cause of temporal happiness and religion
in this land and all over the world."

Herbert Spencer, in a letter to M. Charmes,
one of the reviewers of " The Man *vs*. the State,"
writes :

" If men's sympathies are left to work out naturally, without legal instrumentality, I hold that the
general result will be that the inferior will be sufficiently helped to moderate and alleviate their
miseries, but will not be sufficiently helped to enable them to multiply ; and that so the benefit
will be achieved without the evil."

Lord Derby, in 1879, reasoned :

" Surely it is better to have thirty-five millions
of human beings leading useful and intelligent
lives, rather than forty millions struggling pain-
fully for a bare subsistence."

The ancient philosophers and economists recognized the importance of regulating procreation, for we read in **Aristotle's " Politics,"** Book VII., Chapter 169 : " If the laws of any State prevent exposure of children, that State ought to limit the number of children that any family should bring into the world."

Plato, called " the Divine," in his most famous dialogue, " The Republic," represents his ideal citizens as " not begetting children beyond their means, through a prudent fear of poverty or war." He clearly saw that excessive population causes both poverty and war. History verifies this observation.

Beside these voices of the past may stand the opinion of the great modern, **Charles Darwin,** who wrote :

" There is no exception to the rule that every organic being naturally increases at so high a rate that, if not destroyed, the earth would soon be covered by the progeny of a single pair. Even slow-breeding man has doubled in twenty-five years, and at this rate, in a few thousand years there would literally not be room for his progeny—*i.e,* not *standing* room, as is easily proved by any one acquainted with figures." [1]

---

[1] " The Origin of Species."

We close this series of citations with one from a writer thoroughly familiar with life as it actually is among the masses—**M. M. Pomeroy**. It is a comprehensive summary of the whole question :

" The educated, humane physician who will inform women how to escape compulsory child-bearing will serve God, heaven and taxpayers better than they have been served, lo ! these many years." [1]

In some instances it is absolutely necessary for the health or life of the mother that conception be prevented. Previous child-bearing may have proved that she cannot again undergo the experience without danger.

An eminent authority, **George Napheys, A.M., M.D.,** says on this subject :

" Let us first inquire whether there is such a thing as *over-production*—having *too many* children. Unquestionably there is. Its disastrous effects on both mother and children are known to every intelligent physician. Two-thirds of all cases of womb disease, says Dr. Tilt, are traceable to child-bearing in feeble women. . . . There are also women to whom pregnancy is a nine months'

---

[1] " Pen Pictures of New York Life."

torture, and others to whom it is nearly certain to prove fatal. Such a condition cannot be discovered before marriage. . . . The detestable crime of *abortion* is appallingly rife in our day ; it is abroad in our land to an extent which would have shocked the dissolute women of pagan Rome. . . . This wholesale, fashionable murder, how are we to stop it ? Hundreds of vile men and women in our large cities subsist by this slaughter of the innocent. . . . Their advertisements are seen in the newspapers ; their soul- and body-destroying means are hawked in every town." [1]

Again, a rapid succession of pregnancies is apt to unfit the wife and mother for her duties as such. She becomes prematurely old, and degenerates into nothing but a slave.

Professor H, Newell Martin, in his college textbook upon " The Human Being," writes :

" Many a wife who might have led a long and happy life is made an invalid or brought to premature death through being kept in a chronic state of pregnancy. The professor of gynæcology in a leading medical school gives it as his deliberate opinion that the majority of American women

---

[1] " Physical Life of Women."

must at some periods of their lives choose between freedom from pregnancy and early death."

It is not the fact of a woman's having children
under proper circumstances that ruins her health
and happiness. Womanhood is incomplete without them. She may have a dozen or more and
still have better health than before marriage. It
is in having them too close together and when she
is not in a fit state that her health gives way.
Sometimes it is because of a diseased condition of
the mother that she has children in such rapid
succession. The outlet from the womb, as a result of laceration by a previous child-birth, is frequently enlarged, thus allowing conception to
take place very readily.

Besides the wrong to the mother in having children in such rapid succession, even though every
other circumstance is favorable to the new being,
it is a great injustice to the babe in the womb and
the one at the breast that they should follow each
other so quickly that one is conceived while the
other is nursing. One takes the vitality of the
other ; neither has sufficient nourishment, and
both are started in life stunted and incomplete.

We have now shown that *uncontrolled* procreation is a wrong to the State, a wrong to the fam-

ily, a wrong to the mother, and a wrong to the child itself. If this is so, are we not obliged, by all rules of common-sense and decency, to prevent accidental conception ?

If any argue that the Creator, who made man and beast, intended the same laws to govern the reproduction of both ; that the lower animals propagate without any restriction, and yet they are perfectly healthy ; then let them bear in mind that the lower animals, in their natural state, have sexual intercourse only at certain seasons, and then for propagation only, and not to indulge a lustful appetite. At this time they are in a fit state for another of their species to be conceived, and it is their natural instinct for offspring which prompts their union. They are not diseased, have no evil tendencies to transmit ; and nature, knowing that their lack of reason would prevent their adopting measures to avoid conception, has ordained it so that unlimited numbers can be born to any family without fear of want. Man, on the contrary, is diseased and evil—has born in him abnormal lust and passion, because generation after generation has lived together in ignorance and vice, and he has to provide, no matter what

the odds against him, for whatever family he may
have through the passion he has inherited.

If people were born with only rightful passion
and had strength of character enough to control it,
it might not be necessary, in the majority of cases,
to take measures to prevent conception. However, at present this *is* necessary, for morals cannot be argued or legislated into people ; human
nature has to be taken as it is, not as it ought to
be.   People will have intercourse at all times and
under all circumstances ; and many excuse this
by saying that man has become civilized and cultivated to such an extent that the passion of love
is so strong it must have an outlet in constant
sexual intercourse, regardless of all barriers and
reasons to the contrary.   If this is the case, then
let his civilization, cultivation and love teach
him how to prevent the gratification of his passion
from resulting in a crime.

Some, who reason that nature meant man to
propagate unlimitedly, think it is taking it out of
the Creator's hands to prevent conception.   Man
at present is unnatural and inordinate in his sexual
sphere, and conception as a rule depends not on
the Creator, but on the passion of one or both of
the expectant parents.

One author says, in giving reasons for preventing conception : " Are we not continually thwarting nature ? We are thrust into the world without clothes, and man's devices in the way of raiment protect us from the summer's heat and winter's cold. Nature would, in our climate, freeze us in spite of our clothes, but we build houses over our heads and devise fireplaces, stoves and furnaces to keep us warm. Man's whole life is occupied, one might say, in the work of thwarting nature, or, in other words, in protecting himself against the freaks and severities of nature. We are continually doing it. Nothing, it is often said, is so certain as death ; and the knowing ones who value life are using every device to save themselves from it. Every device of civilization is something to thwart nature, who is as stingy as she is bountiful if we take no means to wrench from her that which we need ; and as bountiful as she is stingy if we do not protect ourselves from her munificence. If we enjoy basking in the glowing and health-giving sunshine, there are times when the greatest lover of nature must protect himself from it ; hence, in July we carry sunshades of some description, or betake ourselves to some cooling shelter. Showers are as necessary as the sun's rays, and we extend our umbrellas above our heads to shelter ourselves from the rain. When the atmosphere stagnates, we use fans to refresh ourselves on a warm summer's day ; and in a variety of ways we seek to alter things to render us more comfortable. There is a tendency among all animals to be too fruitful."

In some large cities, according to **Ryan's** " Philosophy of Marriage," more than one third of the births are out of wedlock. Such children are born steeped in wickedness and disease. Is there not enough crime, disease, suffering and trouble ; are not the institutions for punishment and confinement now too full without making the world any worse than it is by bringing into it more unfortunate beings? If illegal intercourse is carried on to such an alarming extent, and if people will marry, no matter what conditions or circumstances forbid it, then children must follow who are unfit to live or else the parents will resort to abortion. In either case a great wrong has been committed. Would it not be better in such cases never to allow conception to take place?

The following interesting case will serve to illustrate not only the great wrong to a child that it should be misbegotten and the great expense of such to the country, but how entirely inadequate are the means adopted by the government to restrain the reproduction of the low and vicious. The case is that of the Juke family, mostly of New York State, and is related by **Mr. R. L. Dugdale,** when a member of the Prison Association :

" It was traced out by painstaking research that from one woman called Margaret, who, like Topsey, merely ' growed ' without pedigree, as a pauper in a village on the upper Hudson, about eighty-five years ago, there descended 673 children, grandchildren, and great-grandchildren, of whom 200 were criminals of the dangerous class, 280 adult paupers, and 50 prostitutes, while 300 children of her lineage died prematurely. The last fact proves to what extent in this family nature was kind to the rest of humanity in saving it from a still larger aggregation of undesirable and costly members, for it is estimated that the expense to the State of the descendants of Maggie was over a million and a quarter dollars ; and the State itself did something also toward preventing a greater expense by the restraint exercised upon the criminals, paupers and idiots of the family during a considerable portion of their lives."

The following is the opinion of **Dr. Stockham,** as to whether knowledge on this subject is likely to be abused :

" It has been feared that a knowledge of means to prevent conception would, if generally diffused, be abused by women ; that they would to so great an extent escape motherhood as to bring about social disaster. This fear is not well founded. The maternal instinct is inherent and sovereign in women. Even the pre-natal influences of a murderous intent on the part of parents scarcely ever eradicate it. With this natural desire for children, we believe few women would abuse the knowledge or privilege of controlling conception. Although women shrink from forced maternity, and from the bearing of children under the great burden of suffering, as well as other adverse conditions, it is rare to find a woman who is not greatly disappointed if she does not wear the crown of motherhood. Believing in the rights of unborn children and in the maternal instinct, I am consequently convinced that no knowledge should be withheld that will secure proper conditions for the best parenthood.''

There is just as much sin and misery in the world as ever. Are we doing anything to alle-

viate it ? As fast as one wretch is reformed or
one body freed from suffering many more are
born only to fill their place ; and at the present
time none can say whether or not it may be their
child, brother, sister or near one who goes next.
Is this fate necessary ? Most certainly not, for
ordinary people now know how to have only well-
born children ; and if they are so unfortunate as
not to be able to have them, whether from disease
or circumstances, then they, like those who do
not want them and are not fit to be parents, can
find out further on how they may be avoided. For
if it would be " better that a mill-stone were
hanged about one's neck, and that they should
be cast into the sea rather than they should offend
one of these little ones," then a thousand times
more would this be better than that one of these
little ones should be born, through no will of its
own, into this hard, uncharitable world so imperfect that it would early succumb to disease or
vice, and at the best whose life could only be
more or less filled with misery and suffering.
Such children, besides their evil influence, would
in turn become parents ; and so the evil would be
handed on from generation to generation.

CHAPTER III.

Methods.

" Wise men ne'er wail their present woes,
But presently prevent the ways to wail."
—RICHARD II., ACT III.

THE term conception is applied to the process by which the male element contained in the seminal fluid comes in contact with the female ovum, or egg, and fertilizes it. This ovum is so small that it is invisible to the naked eye ; in fact, over one thousand impregnated ova can be placed upon the finger-nail. At the time of menstruation the ovum is thrown off from the ovary, passes along the Fallopian tube to the cavity of the womb, and is here detained for some days. During the generative act the male fluid is deposited in the vagina, and the seminal elements, which have the power of motion, pass up into the womb. It is here that fecundation—that is, fertilization—of the ovum is supposed to take place.

The ovum, in its journey, occupies a time varying from two to fourteen days, and then, if not fecundated, passes away in the excretions. Conception cannot now occur until another ovum starts on its way to the womb, which ordinarily is two weeks later than the fourteenth day from menstruation—that is, at the commencement of the next menstrual flow.

These periods are not fixed and invariable—for instance, conception sometimes occurs during this latter two weeks, when the ovum is not supposed to be present. Probably, in this case, prolonged sexual excitement has hastened the ripening of the ovum, so that it is present for some days before the next menstruation ; or, the elements of the semen, which have a remarkable vitality, may live until the new ovum appears. Again, intercourse during the first two weeks may be unfruitful, for, owing to diseased conditions or other causes, the ovum will pass away from the womb very soon after its arrival there.

These occurrences are infrequent, and the alternate periods of viability and non-viability may be taken as generally reliable. But there are certain women who seem to be especially liable to conceive, no matter at what time during the intermenstrual period the act takes place. For these

and for those parents who find the above plan in-
effectual, other means are necessary.

It is much to be regretted that a chapter giving
entirely effectual and satisfactory, yet not in the
least harmful, methods for preventing conception
will have to be omitted, owing to a bill rushed
through in the last moments of a recent Con-
gressional session by a few misled, self-styled
moralists. This bill makes it unlawful to publish
any matter on this subject. We did not learn
of this until just before publication. Truly has
de La Bruyere said :

> " If Poverty is the Mother of Crimes,
> Want of Sense is the Father."

It is to be hoped the time is not far distant
when progress toward the attainment of better
physique, higher happiness and more prosperity
for man will not be interfered with ; when the people will have liberty and freedom as to what they
shall or shall not read or discuss, and when all
will be possessed of a knowledge which will prevent the large per cent of those unfortunates now
born weak, imperfect or diseased from ever
being conceived.

Conclusion.

" When the best wisdom of the race, expressing and enforcing itself in a rational way, shall be able to stand at the entrance frontier of human life, and say who shall pass, it will have the key to open for mankind the better era, the good time coming of the popular thought, the republic of which Plato speculated, the Utopia of Thomas More, and the Arcadia of Sir Philip Sydney."

" Better to be unborn than untaught : for ignorance is the root
of misfortune."—PLATO.

" When the *judgment's weak,*
The prejudice is strong."
                                        —KANE O'HARA.

PART III.

HYGIENE AND PHYSIOLOGY OF GENERATIVE LIFE.

CHAPTER I.

Introductory.

" The great obstacle to progress is prejudice."—Bovee.

PHYSIOLOGY teaches that in the proper exercise of any natural faculty or propensity in man, there is nothing that is impure, low, sensualizing or in any way degrading. Then is it not high time that true hygiene and physiology of the generative system should be taught to all? For the amount of misery, disease and crime resulting from the ignorant use of these organs is appalling, and few would give credit to its alarming extent.

Ignorance is not necessarily innocence, and it is the height of folly to be ignorant on this subject.

Can the young or the old be heedless of what goes on around them ; can the young, no matter of what tender years, be deaf to the obscene language of servants and playmates ; or can they be blind to the evil practices by which they are surrounded, and by which they are at any time liable to be contaminated ?

Is it possible that parents will attempt to deny that *their* sons and daughters are liable to such evil, or that a great responsibility rests on them to do all in their power to correct it ? Are there any so overcome by mock modesty or so narrow-minded and ignorant as to wish to remain in darkness on this question ; or any who do not think that all, except the very young, should be enlightened, to some extent at least, in these essential matters ?

The mere fact of any woman having Mrs. prefixed to her name tells to all the world that she lives, or has lived, according to the marriage relation ; and furthermore that she is a mother, or will be, if she is a true woman, unless diseased or deformed. To the right-minded, marriage in all its relations is most sacred and pure ; and a virtuous, intelligent woman must have thought so or she would not have demoralized herself by entering

that state.   Then, granting that the married state
is a holy one, and that " to the pure all things
are pure," does it not follow conclusively that she
or he who does not want to live in a natural,
proper way, according to the divine laws, and
have only well-born children, is either too ignorant to marry at all or too degraded to belong to
any class of society ?

It is not enough that one should be virtuous
one's self ; a man of virtue will be a friend of virtue, and, according to his influence and ability,
will he see that all are possessed of a rightful
knowledge on this vital subject.   Truly the ways
of wisdom " are ways of pleasantness, and all her
paths are peace."

Nowhere does knowledge mean so much, because here it materially influences morals, public
health, population, disease, mortality, besides personal reputation, property and even life itself.
The responsibility for diffusing knowledge on this
subject rests on all, but especially on those in
political power, those of wealth and influence
and on none more heavily than ministers and
physicians.

It is our purpose to accompany the human being
through all the phases of generative life.   Begin-

ning with early childhood and continuing th ough puberty to full maturity, we will outline the dangers to which it is exposed and the care tl at it requires. We will then take up the subject of marriage, dealing with the health, age and temperament of the contracting parties. The events of married life will then be discussed, including generation, the control of the passions, sterility and prevention of infection, and hygiene of pregnancy.

CHAPTER II.

Hygiene of Generative Life from Childhood to Maturity.

" So dear to heaven is saintly chastity,
    That when a soul is found sincerely so,
    A thousand hovered angels lackey her,
    Driving far off each thing of sin and guilt."
                                    —MILTON.

IN the first part of this book we have demonstrated how to have well-born children; but whether well born or not, it is necessary that the generative system should be properly attended to.

For this purpose it must be understood that a child's mind is most flexible and susceptible of impression, early impressions generally continuing to old age.

Every possible care should be taken to keep it from evil influences and baneful habits. Even infants at the breast, whose sexual organs are so imperfectly developed and who can have no sexual desire whatever, often contract the habit of touching and playing with these parts. It is a very common thing for children from the age of one and two years to play with these organs and form most injurious habits. This is easily explained by physiology, in that the generative organs are lined by similar mucous membrane to that of the mouth, stomach, bowels and other organs ; and when irritation is set up at any point, any other part of the body covered or lined with this membrane may become deranged. There are many causes for this irritation, such as improper food, teething, worms and cold ; and there are few infants who do not suffer from one of these, the result being inflammation and irritation of the generative as well as of other organs. Every mother has seen erections in the male infant from the pressure of urine in the bladder or from any physical irritation of the parts ; and while female infants do not show it, they are just as liable to this excitement. Children of all ages, with rare exception, are fed in such a way that they are prone to develop permanent congestion and constant irritation of the pelvic organs, and so precocious and entirely morbid amativeness results. Tea, coffee, meats, highly flavored confectionery, spices, stimulants and pickles account for much of this early tendency to impurity.

One writer says on this subject : " One of the most effective of the exciting causes (of masturbation) is wrong dietetic habits.   That a child—as thousands are—can be fed on highly seasoned and gross food—lard, eggs, pastry, animal food, pepper, salt, candies, pickles, tea, coffee, etc., and, as very many are, on some form or other of alcoholic liquors—and not have amative desires is utterly impossible.   Feeding with such food as gravies, pies, tea and coffee to a five- or ten-year-old angel from heaven would produce in it a tendency to self-abuse, avoiding all mention of a child of the earth, born with an inherited tendency."

From an early age, children are exposed to the danger of contamination from immoral, profane and obscene ideas from playmates or servants— for many of the latter are morally corrupt ; and it seems as if this class took especial delight in poisoning the minds of the young and innocent and initiating them into habits of vice.   While children often contract evil from playmates, it is as nothing when compared with that wrought by immoral servants, and when the children grow up, most severely do they censure them ; and also the parents for their negligence.   None will deny that it is right that the young should know, to a certain extent, something of the generative organs ; but is it right, is it wise, is it safe, is it not ruinous to the best interests of mankind that the discussion of this subject should be left to those of corrupt morals ?

While the vice among all classes of adults is bad enough, for this state of immorality to exist among children is appalling ; and it seems all the more so because parents and guardians, who might prevent it by explaining and entering into their children's lives, leave the subject untouched. If boys and girls do not get this knowledge from one source they will from another ; and so it devolves upon the base and immoral to initiate them into sin and vice. This applies to both sexes ; and if any parents believe their children incapable of immorality, let them investigate, and they will be astounded and dismayed at the probable lack of purity in their sons and daughters.

Children are not responsible for coming into the world ; it is upon the parents that this rests, and it is for the parents to care for them while they are young and incapable, and give them no cause to curse them when they grow up because they did not guard them from evil. This is their bounden duty, and not only of the parents, but of all those who have the guardianship and instruction of youth.

If children were taught to eat, drink, dress and exercise hygienically ; were given enough to do— for truly idleness is the mother of evil ; and had good influences in their homes, not neglecting the higher culture, they would never form habits of vice. Fill a child full of good, and there will be no room for the evil.

Once such habits are formed, it is exceedingly difficult to break them. The best means to eradicate this evil are moral restraint, physical exertion even to fatigue, open-air amusement, active mental employment and plain, unstimulating food and drink.

Even young children should not be allowed to sleep together, for besides the tendency to immorality this might have, it is harmful physically.

Too great care cannot be taken to keep them from evil influence ; for a base, obscene person in society is a moral leper whose touch is degradation and whose breath is contamination. Every child should be taught, as they are able to understand it, the proper care and use of the generative organs ; for a rightful knowledge of this subject at an early age would be the earthly salvation of thousands.

Puberty.

At this period the generative organs suddenly and rapidly develop ; all characteristics of childhood disappear ; the girls ripen into womanhood, the boys into manhood. In girls, it occurs from the age of thirteen to fifteen ; in boys, from fourteen to sixteen ; but it takes the latter longer to develop. This is a most critical period, for the child is now extremely susceptible to influence. As **Aristotle** says, " Puberty insures health or deranges it ; the body becomes thin or full ; delicate children become robust and strong children become delicate ; many diseases disappear, others are developed."

From the maturing of the generative organs and the amorous impulse at this time, touching and manipulating are almost instinctively developed. A child indulging in this artificial excitation is in the greatest danger of contracting the baneful habit of masturbation, or self-pollution ; and this becomes almost a certainty if it has had bad habits previous to puberty.

Such vice becomes really a disease, and unless checked must be the ruination of the child in mind and body. If such cases were rare it would be bad enough, but as this habit is a most frequent one it is appalling.

The parents' weight of responsibility at this time is tremendous, for a child without a parent's loving guidance during this critical period is in a worse state than a ship without a pilot, in a storm among rocks and hidden shoals.

The inseparable relation of moral and physical structure is seen at this age ; and it is the greatest fallacy to separate mind and body in educational arrangements.

Dr. Ellis has dealt so efficiently with this subject that we quote the following from him :

" The time has been, perhaps, when there was safety to the young in ignorance, or at least that it was properly left to teachers and parents to guard children and the young in this respect ; but an observation of many years has satisfied me that, at present, there is no safety except from the general diffusion of knowledge on this subject ; for few children, especially boys in our country, arrive at an age when they would be likely to take up this volume to read who do not know all about this vice. It is taught by vicious associates or accidentally acquired. Strong hereditary inclination to an abuse of this propensity may have something to do with this perversion. Parents are not aware of the signs by which this vice can be detected, nor of the terrible consequences which follow this unnatural practice, and especially that young children, even as young as from four to six years and upward, may be the victims, and destroy health, reason and even life at this early age. In fact, it is sometimes taught by nurses to children even younger than four years. So that it is all important that parents be instructed upon this subject, and be constantly upon the watch.

" ' There is a number of children of both sexes,' says **Dr. Teste,** in his work on the ' Diseases of Children,' ' who are liable to contract this habit at the age of four, five, or even three years. . . . The first sentiment that this species of sensuality awakens in children is a sort of bashfulness incompatible with the innocence of their age. . . . The bashfulness of a child of ten years is always suspicious.'

" The young child, of course, should be kept ignorant of this subject, if practicable, as long as possible, unless by watchfulness the parent is satisfied that he is addicted to the practice ; but the youngest child should never be allowed to take any liberties with his organs of generation ; and a nurse who is guilty of thus abusing a child should be dismissed forthwith and severely reprimanded.   The child should be taught from the first that it is very wrong, immodest and wicked to handle the parts ; so that he may be prepared to shun this evil when he comes to know of its existence, which he is very sure to do, from vicious associates, if not from the vulgar insinuations or allusions of adults.   As it is desirable that parents and teachers should be able to detect the existence of this vice in children and in young persons, in order to warn them against it, I will give the most important signs by which this habit is manifested. If we notice a child, or a young gentleman or lady, who has usually been healthy and bright or intelligent beginning to look delicate, pale-faced or bloodless, with sunken, ghastly eyes, with or even without, dark, semicircular lines beneath the eyes, with redness of the edges of the eyelids, with a dull, heavy, sleepy look of the eyes ; if there is a clammy, greasy feel of the skin, especially of the palms of the hands ; if there is weakness in the small of the back, with more or less pain ; if the ends of the hair are split, the appetite variable ; if many of the above symptoms exist, we have a right to suspect that the child or adult is addicted to this vice ; and if, instead of the frank, open stare of childhood or the more modest look of youth, the eyes are averted when they meet ours, especially if the individual is of the same sex ; if the mind is listless, dull, stupid, forgetful, without the joyous playfulness of childhood and youth ; if there is great and unusual irritability of temper, amounting to peevishness ; absent-mindedness, sadness, melancholy, unusual fearfulness, with indecision in his movements—if many of these symptoms exist, together with some of those first named, we have almost positive evidence that the individual is addicted to this habit. Sexual excesses may give rise to many of these symptoms. Coffee drinking may cause some of them in children, and novel-reading and idleness in young ladies ; but this vice is exceedingly common in connection with these bad habits. When any considerable number of the above symptoms, especially any of those about the eyes or of the mental symptoms exist, it is the duty of the parent, guardian or teacher to ascertain by careful inquiries if the child or young person is not addicted to this habit. As it is very desirable that

young children—say under ten or twelve years—
who are ignorant of this practice, should be kept
so, it is better to watch them carefully than to
speak to them openly about it until we are satisfied. If at this young age we carefully watch
the child's actions, we shall soon discover that the
genital organs attract an unusual share of the
child's attention if he or she is addicted to this
vice.

" A young child can only be broken of this practice by constant watchfulness during the day
until he goes to sleep at night, and requiring him
to arise the moment he awakes in the morning ;
and in inveterate cases it may be necessary that
a night dress preventing the hands passing below
the waist be worn during the night, and the child
never be allowed to be out of sight during the day.
This will require care and much trouble ; but
parents should remember that the child inherits,
most likely, a predisposition to a perversion of this
propensity from them, and that the health, reason and life of their offspring are at stake, and,
perhaps, the avoidance of diseases far worse than
death, if possible, depends upon their faithfulness ;
for epilepsy, hysteria, insanity and idiocy, when
they occur between the third and thirtieth years,

arise without much doubt more frequently from this habit than from all other causes whatever put together.

" This vice is often taught children by nurses, servants and older persons, as has already been intimated, but it is more frequently communicated from one child to another. A single boy may corrupt others. **Sylvester Graham,** in his lectures to young men, says :

" ' The most fruitful sources of instruction in this vice are vicious associates—especially in boarding-schools and colleges. The extent to which this evil prevails, and of the mischief resulting from it, in most of these institutions is perhaps beyond credibility ; and none but those who have thoroughly investigated this subject can have any just apprehensions of the difficulties in preventing it. The utmost care and vigilance and precautionary measures have sometimes failed to keep it out of public institutions for the instruction of the youth. It is enough to make a parent's heart recoil with horror when he contemplates the danger to which his child is exposed on becoming a member of some of these institutions. And they are greatly deceived who suppose that a majority of the boys who enter these institutions escape the contamina-

tion ! . . . The common notion that boys are
generally ignorant in relation to this matter, and
that we ought not to remove that ignorance, is
wholly incorrect. I am confident that I speak
within bounds when I say that seven out of every
ten boys in our country at the age of twelve have
at least heard of this pernicious practice, and I
say, again, the extent to which it prevails in our
schools and colleges is shocking beyond measure !
I have known boys to leave some of these institutions at the age of twelve and thirteen, almost entirely ruined in health and constitution by it, and
they have assured me that to their certain knowledge almost every boy in the school practised the
filthy vice.'

" I have also known this vice taught to a school-
room full of girls at one time. Our long school
hours and want of systematic exercise for the
young predispose to this vice by begetting debility
and nervous irritability, instead of vigorous health.
And when, in addition to all this, a parent allows
his children, or young men or women, to eat
freely of meat, especially highly-seasoned meat, or
that containing any pepper or other spices, mus-
tard, horseradish, or other stimulating ingredi-
ents, or to use coffee, tea, or wine, if they do not

acquire this vice simply from pruriency, whether taught it or not, it will not be his fault, for he will have certainly done all in his power to predispose to it. And if when they become young men and women he allows them to continue the use of such unnatural stimulants, and to live a student's life, without proper exercise, and to read the yellow-covered literature of the day, if they rush into licentiousness, as well as continue this solitary vice ; and also into dissipation, and thus destroy both body and soul, he may thank himself for their destruction, and blame no one else ; for the causes which he has voluntarily permitted to operate, perhaps instituted, are only producing their legitimate effects upon his children ; and he has no right to expect any other result than their destruction, and they will owe few thanks to him if this does not ensue.

"But in regard to the particular form of vice we are now considering, a distinguished lady, in her 'Lectures to Ladies on Anatomy and Physiology,' says :

" ' There is reason to believe that in nine cases out of ten, those unhappy females who are tenants of houses of ill fame have been victims to this vice in the first place. Were this the peculiar vice of the low and vulgar, there might be more excuse for the apathy and false delicacy that pervade the community respecting it ; but it invades all ranks. Professed Christians are among its victims.'

" **William C. Woodbridge,** in the ' Annals of Education,' writes in regard to the subject of this chapter :

" ' A topic in physiology which artificial modesty has covered until a solitary but fatal vice is spreading desolation throughout our schools and families, unnoticed and unknown.'

" **Dr. Woodward** says that those who hold the opinion that information on this subject is unnecessary or injurious ' are hardly aware how extensively known this habit is with the young, or how early in life it is sometimes practised.   I have never conversed with a lad twelve years of age who did not know all about the practice, and understand the language commonly used to describe it.'

" **E. M. R. Wells,** a celebrated teacher in Boston, says : ' Thousands of pure-minded and amiable boys and young men are undermining their physical constitutions and prospectively corrupting their souls by a pleasurable, and, to many of them, an innocent gratification '—innocent be-

cause ignorantly practised, without being aware
that it is destroying them or is sinful. How important, then, that parents not only understand this
subject, but that they watch their children while
young, and give the needed instructions as they
grow older !

" This habit is a fruitful cause of consumption in
the young, as it impairs the organs of nutrition
and secretion. It not only predisposes to this
disease, but also to scrofulous diseases, spinal dis-
tortions, etc. It also causes impotency and disease and wasting of the testicles in the male ; and
ovarian disease, leucorrhœa and profuse menstruation with the female. But the effects of this vice
cease not with the individuals who practise it,
but are visited upon their children, in the form of
a feeble constitution, which renders them more
liable to suffer and die from the diseases of childhood ; or if they survive to manhood, they are
feeble, dyspeptic and spend a miserable existence
unless the utmost pains are taken during childhood and youth and continued during manhood
to develop the organism. This habit also, by im-
pairing the vigor and vitality of the system, renders the individual far more liable to be attacked
by any inflammatory or epidemic disease, and far

more liable to die of such disease, than an individual of good habits.

" **Dr. Adam Clarke** says in regard to this vice :

" ' It is one of the most destructive evils ever practised by fallen man.   In many respects it is several degrees worse than common whoredom, and it has in its train more awful consequences. It excites nature to undue action and produces violent secretions, which necessarily and speedily exhaust the vital principle and energy ; hence the muscles become flaccid and feeble, the tone and natural action of the nerves relaxed and impeded, the understanding confused, the memory oblivious, the judgment perverted, the will indeterminate, and wholly without energy to resist ; the eyes appear languishing and without expression, and the countenance vacant ; the appetite ceases, for the stomach is incapable of performing its proper office ; nutrition fails ; tremors, fears and terrors are generated ; and thus the wretched victim drags out a miserable existence, till superannuated, even before he had time to arrive at man's estate, with a mind often debilitated even to a state of idiotism, his worthless body tumbles into his grave.'

'' So far as the physical and mental consequences

are concerned, the above is a fair picture of the results which follow in extreme cases ; and if the
practice is knowingly followed, with a full com-
prehension of the guilt and consequence, it is
morally true ; but as this practice is often followed
by the young ignorantly they are comparatively
innocent, even more so than their parents, who,
through ignorance—which is less excusable at this
day—or heedlessness have neglected to warn them
of the dangers to which they are so subject.   All
that can be expected of the young person is to
cease this practice as soon as he is aware that it is
wrong.   To continue it after this, it becomes to
him a sin.   It is surprising how soon the physical
and mental effects of this vice will often disappear when the child or young person ceases entirely this habit.   Sometimes there is an irritable
state of the genital organs remaining after the
vice has been put away, causing emissions during
sleep, accompanied with lascivious dreams, which
may keep up the mental and physical symptoms
to some extent ; but by a proper course these
symptoms will gradually pass away and health
generally be restored, provided the individual
keeps away from quacks and advertised quack
medicines, which rarely fail to do harm in the

end, as these remedies are generally stimulants.
Let a patient thus affected restrain his thoughts
from all lascivious subjects, which may be difficult at first, but if he perseveringly strives he will
succeed in the end ; let him avoid reading aught
that excites this passion, take regular active exercise in the open air and sun ; also in the gymna-
sium, if living in a village or city, or work on a
farm, if in the country.   In regard to diet, let him
attend to the following suggestions by **Dr. Woodward:**

"'The regimen must be strict : the diet should
be simple and nutritious, and sufficient in quantity ;
it should be rather plain than light and abstemious ;
no stimulating condiments should be used ; the
suppers should be particularly light and late suppers should be wholly avoided.   All stimulating
drinks, even strong tea and coffee, should be dis-
carded ; cider and wine are very pernicious ; tobacco in all its forms not less so.'

"'As for suppers,' says **Mr. Fowler,** to whose
work I have referred, 'I prefer none at all ;'
certainly they should be very light and never late.
Let him think as little as possible about this afflic-
tion, for multitudes who enjoy comparative health
are troubled in the same way occasionally, there-

fore do not despair if the difficulty is not overcome
entirely at once, for it may require years for this ;
but the discharges will become less and less frequent, and the effects upon mind and body, if the
individual persevere, will gradually pass off, especially if he cultivates cheerfulness and engages
in timely and proper amusements, and does not
allow his mind to be harassed by useless regrets
for the past, which are neither required by reason
nor revelation. His whole duty, so far as this
matter is concerned, is to cease to do evil and
learn to be well, be contented, and leave the result with the Divine Providence.

" It has been my aim to say no more than seems
absolutely necessary to arouse parents and teachers to a sense of their duty to the young, and to
warn all, for I know that parents are either very
ignorant of the dangers to which their children
are exposed or culpably negligent ; for so far as
my observation extends, few parents ever caution
their children against this vice, or warn and restrain them after they have commenced it. The
subject is a delicate one, but that does not justify
a neglect of duty, and many a child has felt this,
and has in anguish of soul exclaimed, as he has
been suffering the consequences of such neg-

lect in after years, ' Oh, why did not my parents warn me of the danger from this habit ! Then I might have been saved from destruction.' Let no parent flatter himself that his children, however carefully he has trained them, however good, kind and modest, are exempt from a liability to this vice ; in fact, excessive modesty or bashfulness is a suspicious symptom, and may well lead the parent to increased watchfulness, for he will be very likely to find its true cause in this bad practice. Let the parent watch his children while very young, and when they get to be old enough to have some judgment, warn them against the evil example and teachings of others, or place in their hands some proper book, which shall give them the needed instruction and warning. Your child has curiosity and instinct, and there are no objections to his knowing correctly the true use of every part of his organization early—not while too young ; be his teacher, then, if not directly, at least through the instrumentality of proper books ; for if you do not teach him correctly the use and dangers resulting from abuse, others will teach him the abuses without pointing out the danger which results. Then teach the use and warn against the abuse, and through constant watchful-

ness guard well the impressible being committed
to your charge.   And especially teach your children and the young that this vice and every form
of licentiousness are sins against God, and that
as such they must shun these evils.'

CHAPTER III.

Physical Essentials for Marriage.

" Though fools spurn Hymen's gentle powers,
  We, who improve his golden hours,
    By sweet experience know
  That marriage, *rightly understood*,
  Gives to the tender and the good
    A paradise below."
                                    —COTTON.

HAVING followed the child in its generative life
through childhood, puberty and adolescence, we are
now prepared to discuss the subject of marriage.

It is necessary that those engaging in marriage
should be of sound health, of a proper age, should
have the means to support a family and, lastly,
but more important than all, that they should be
well mated, for without this it would be the height
of folly to think of getting married—at least as far
as children are concerned.

Health.

It is most essential for those entering this state
to be sound in body and mind, because nature has
ordained it that from the union of two a third

should come ; and as its welfare in body and mind depends on the parents, it would be wrong to enter the marriage state so unhealthy that this third being would suffer and be handicapped during its entire existence.

Just as it would be the greatest folly to plant a diseased or damaged grain of corn, expecting to reap good grain, so it would be with sowing the seeds for a new being.   For this and other reasons it is necessary that there should be a standard which people should approach before entering the matrimonial state.

Nature meant that only the finest, strongest, most beautiful, and only those of most spirit, energy and brains should mate.   This is shown among the lower animals in their natural state, and was true of the ancients ; but in modern times, any one and every one marries, regardless of their condition and of all reason.   If children did not result from such unions, little harm would be done ; however, if people who are unfit to become parents will marry, then let them avoid conceiving children.   Just as a certain form of nose, for instance, can be traced through twenty generations and more, so can parents, if unsound, entail curses on generation after generation.

Thus it is essential for expectant parents to know that they should not marry if they are diseased, have an uncontrollable appetite for alcoholic liquors, or if contaminated with insanity or scrofulous constitution to any great extent, or if they suffer from causeless or excessive melancholy. Neither should two marry who have a tendency to the same disease, or who are blood relations. Furthermore, even if a man does not intend to have children, he should not marry if he has any disease with which his wife could become infected.

Age and Circumstances.

These are important factors as to marriage. Premature and late as well as ill-assorted marriages are highly injurious to the procreation of vigorous, healthy offspring, and to public morality.

Early Marriages.—Not only are very early marriages injurious to offspring, but they are harmful to the parents, for precocious sexual intercourse greatly debilitates the moral, intellectual and physical powers of both sexes, shortens life, and predisposes the female to miscarriage and disease. Acting on the impulse of headstrong caprice and passion, young persons too often prematurely rush thoughtlessly and

blindly into engagements which in after life become matters of painful regret.   The fairy visions
of love's paradise then vanish, and the sober reali-
ties of life—its cares, its difficulties, and its positive evils—soon lead to discontent, constant repining, and worse than all, to a growing mutual in-
difference.   Such cases are not rare ; every day
we see those at the head of families who are little
more than boys and girls, who need discretion to
direct themselves.   Love cannot clothe, educate
or maintain a family, nor yet satisfy the impor-
tunity of a distressed or impatient creditor.   What
folly it is, then, to marry when too young without
sufficient means ; and worse than the reckless, it
is often the degraded and vicious who take this
step, much to the detriment of their progeny, for
many children result from such marriages.

It is almost impossible to fix an age under which
marriage should not take place.   Circumstances
alter cases ; but there are few instances where
men should marry under twenty-three and few
where women should marry under twenty.   In
nearly every instance it would be detrimental to
their own welfare and that of their posterity.

In some countries the law renders it illegal for
any young man to marry under the age of twenty-

five, or any young woman before she is eighteen ; and every man must show that he has the means to support a family.   It is to be hoped that the time is not far off when this will be a general law, and will be extended to prevent the diseased, the infirm and incapable, if not from marrying, at least from having children.

However, while it is wrong to marry too young, it is best not to put it off too long, for truly " hope deferred maketh the heart sick ;" and when marriage is unreasonably delayed, the heart, losing the elasticity of youthful ardor and hope, becomes blunted by the disappointments and vexations of life, and is seldom the subject of disinterested love and genuine affection.   Tastes, habits and feelings become settled, and they are little disposed to accommodate themselves to the peculiarities of others.

Late Marriages.—There is just as much to be said against the late as against the premature marriage.   If elderly people marry with the intention of not having children, little harm will result ; but it is the greatest mistake for a man, whose physical powers are declining, to beget a child, for vigorous offspring cannot result.

It is impossible to fix a limit beyond which mar-

riage should not be engaged in. It depends entirely on the individual and concerns mostly men,
as women very seldom marry after forty, and
rarely bear children when over forty-five ; while
men frequently marry late in life, and it is not
at all impossible for a man to be the father of a
child—such as it is—when he is in quite advanced
years.

Some men age much more quickly than others ;
but no man who is in old age—that is, who is not
in the full vigor of health—should marry, expecting to become a parent, nor should such a one
who is already married beget offspring.

Temperaments.

The next and most important consideration in
marriage is the mating of the temperaments. This
is really the foundation of marriage, for true love
cannot exist where those concerned in the union
are not at heart somewhat adapted to each other.
Love is the natural sympathy between two who
are suited to each other, and is the unseen but
ever-working force which tends to bring together
the right parties to a marriage union.

As one writer has well expressed it : " A chemist in his laboratory stands holding two vessels,

one in each hand. The two liquids which they contain he pours into a third vessel, and forthwith a new substance appears. With keen and thorough penetration he knows the laws of the interaction of the forces in the two liquids, in what proportions they will combine and what they will produce. Such thoroughly masterful knowledge and work is called scientific chemistry.

"Two lives are to be poured together into the supreme containing vessel which nature has provided, and it may be or may not be a new life is to appear. Is not a new life of a higher order and of more value than aught which can ever appear in the chemist's cup? And is it not befitting to men endowed with the power of self-conscious knowledge and appointed to the mastery of nature's deepest secrets, that they shall acquire as thorough a knowledge of those forces of life by the union of which a new life is to appear, as the chemist has with regard to the chemicals in his cups, or at least that they shall make all possible effort thereunto? This new and most sacred chemistry of life, in its interior and secret laws for the reproduction of life, is what all should know."

The term "temperament" means a state of the body with respect to the predominance of any

single quality ; for instance, if one has a predominance of the vital organs, he would be classed as
of the vital temperament ; if the brain and nervous
system predominated, he would be of the encephal-
ic or nervous temperament ; and if the bone and
muscle system predominated, he would be of the
bony or motive temperament.   These are generally combined in every individual, but in varying
proportions.   Sometimes one temperament is ex-
cessively developed and the others are deficient, or
two may predominate and the others be deficient.

The physical and mental powers depend as to
their development on one or other of these temperaments.   If the brain is in excess, that one will
be strongest mentally ; if the bones and muscles
are in excess, then the physical powers will be
most prominent, and so on.   If all the temperaments are developed, the whole system will be
strong.   Nature intended that when two unite
they should balance up each other's weakness and
deficiencies so as to form one perfect whole ; and
this is of such vital importance that when disregarded marriage is more or less a failure, according to the extent of the discord.   Not only is the
happiness of the contracting parties concerned,
but also the welfare of their offspring in body and

soul, for generation after generation may be made to suffer disease, misery and imperfection from one discordant union.

If two should marry who are precisely alike in temperament their union would be sterile. Washington and Napoleon are instances of this, they both being childless, as their wives were of the same temperament as themselves.

Dr. Jacques, in his excellent little work on the temperaments, has given some very valuable suggestions on marriage. He says :

" Some physiologists have taught that the constitution of the parties in marriage should be similar, so as to insure similar tastes, habits and modes of thought ; while others have contended that contrasts should be sought to give room for variety, and prevent the stagnation of a level sameness. Neither of these statements expresses fully the true law of selection, though both are partly true. There can be no harmony without a difference ; but there may be a difference without harmony. It is not that she is like him that a man loves a woman, but because she is unlike. For the same reason she loves him. The qualities which the one lacks are those which in the other attract and hold the fancy and the heart. The more womanly the woman, the greater her power over men ; and in proportion as she approaches the masculine in person or in character, will she repel the other sex ; while a woman admires no less in man true manliness, and feels for effeminacy and weakness in him either pity or contempt. What should be sought, and what is sought, as a rule, in a husband or wife, where arbitrary conventional customs and considerations of rank, wealth and positions are not allowed to interfere, is not a counterpart but a complement—something to supply a lack—the other self, which shall round out one's being and form a perfect, symmetrical whole. As in music it is not contiguous notes which combine to form chords, but those separated from each other, as a first, and a third, and a fifth ; so we produce social and domestic harmony by associating graduated differences. Two persons may be ' too much alike to agree.' They crowd each other, for ' two objects cannot occupy the same space at the same time.' So, while a ' union of opposites ' is by no means to be insisted upon, or even recommended as a rule, yet a too close similarity in constitution should be avoided, as detrimental to offspring as well as inimical to the happiness of the parties themselves.

Mental Temperament.—'' The mental temperament, for instance, strongly developed in both,
would tend to intensify the intellectual activity
already, perhaps, too great in each ; and if offspring should unfortunately result, they would
be likely to inherit in still greater excess the
constitutional tendencies of the parents.

'' In the same way a marked preponderance of
the motive or vital systems in both parents leads
to a similar state of connubial discord and a lack
of temperamental balance in the children, if any
resulted from the union.   Where there is a close
approximation to a symmetrical and harmonious
development—a balance of temperaments—the
union of similar organizations is less objectionable,
and may result favorably as respects both parents
and children ; but such cases are so rare that a
rule drawn from them would prove of little practical value.

Vital Temperament.—'' The vital system is
the life-giving and life-sustaining element in
the human constitution, and must be considered
as the physical basis of marriage and parent-
age.   This temperamental element should, therefore, undoubtedly be strongly indicated in one
or other of the parties to a union, and if strik-

ingly deficient in one, should be predominant in the other to insure a proper balance of offspring. A man with an excess of the mental temperament and deficient in vital stamina should either remain single or marry a woman with an immense fund of vitality, but sufficiently intellectual to appreciate him, share in a degree his aspirations and sympathize with him in his tastes. If he were to marry a woman of the mental temperament and of low vitality, the children if any would probably be few and puny and die young ; the too keen sensibilities, the excess of mental activity, and the intensity of all the pains they suffer, or the pleasures they enjoy, would soon wear out the inadequate physical system with which alone their parents were able to endow them.

Motive Temperament.—"Where the motive temperament is strongly indicated, there is needed in the one selected as 'partner for life' a predominance of the vital or nutritive system to impart vivacity and cheerfulness to the family circle, and to transmit to offspring the proper degree of mental and physical activity, warmth, amiability and suavity of character, as well as to give a desirable softness and plumpness to the physical system ; while a good development of the mental is requisite to refine and give intellectual power and æsthetic tastes.

" A man with a strongly developed motive temperament united in marriage to a woman of the same organization, would lack the stimulating, warming and softening influences which so favorably modify the somewhat slow, cold, rough, hard and austere features characteristic of that constitution ; the pair would move too slowly for the current of progress around them unless awakened by the strong influence of some grand revolutionary movement ; and their children would inherit in a still higher degree their homely angularities and their energetic, persistent and sturdy, but hard, rough and severe traits of character. Fortunately the motive temperament is not a common one among women, nor do men of this organization affect their style of beauty, even in its modified feminine form, but look rather for the plump rosiness of the fair-haired blonde, or the pale, delicate loveliness of the gray-eyed Psyche, whose frailness appeals to their strength and whose mental quickness contrasts so strongly with their slow but powerful intellectual movements.

" A rational, natural and harmonious marriage connection requires to have its foundation laid in a broad, full vitality ; but this element must not compromise also the superstructure. Where both parties are of the vital temperament, the union is not favorable either to them or to their children ; there being no cooling, refining influence at work with them, the parents are apt to give way too much to their impulses and passions, to live too fast, to fall into excesses and dissipations, be fitful, vacillating and indolent, and to transmit to their children too much of the animal nature, too little mental power and an excess of appetite, passion, and love of pleasure. An influential development of the mental and the motive elements in a husband or wife should be sought by a person of a full vital temperament, the one to give toughness and the other to refine and elevate the character and impart intellectuality, taste and love of culture to offspring.

" From the foregoing considerations, it appears that the point to be aimed at is a proper balance in all the temperamental elements, what is lacking in the husband to be made up in the wife and *vice versa*, the one being a complement or counterpoise of the other, so that an even development, as nearly as possible, may be transmitted to offspring.

" Beyond the somewhat general statements thus made, the correctness of which can hardly be called in question, it is not, perhaps, in the present state of our knowledge of the laws of social harmony safe to go. We have correctly given, as we believe, the general law of harmony in our social relations. If we cannot lay down exact formulæ for its practical application, which will apply to all cases, it is simply because the gamut of the human passions, unlike that of the musical notes, has not been definitely determined, or the elements of our physical organization reduced to a graduated series. The time will come, in the progress of the race in knowledge, when men will touch with no uncertain fingers the keys which are to render the sublime anthem of disenthralled and harmonized humanity. In the mean time, reader, first ' know thyself,' mentally and temperamentally, and then through the ' signs of character '—as stamped upon every organization—upon the cranium, upon the face, upon every organ, feature and movement, study and become acquainted with those around you, and you will find little difficulty in determining, in reference to any particular individual of the opposite sex, whether

there is between you and him, or her, that graduated difference that might bring harmony out of
union."

> " What is there in the vale of life
>   Half so delightful as a wife,
>   When friendship, love and peace combine
>   To stamp the marriage bond divine ?
>   The stream of pure and genuine love
>   Derives its current from above ;
>   And earth a second Eden shows
>   Where'er the healing water flows."
>
> —COWPER.

CHAPTER IV.

Events of Married Life.

" Moderation is the silken string running
Through the pearl chain of all virtues."
—FULLER.

WE have given the essentials for a well-mated
marriage, but whether well mated or not, people
will marry, and so it is necessary that these and all
married people should be informed as to the hygiene
of the generative system, else through ignorance
they and their progeny will suffer disastrous consequences. The average couple is densely ignorant
as to the proper exercise of the marital relations.
With the great mass of the people, sexual intercourse is a morbid appetite, indulged to a large
extent from ignorance, just as a gluttonous appetite
is indulged for alcoholic liquors, food or tobacco.
Husbands through over-indulgence are responsible, though it may be ignorantly, for about half
the uterine troubles which so afflict womankind.
This is why so many women improve more readi-

ly when away from home, at health resorts, sani-
tariums, etc.

One writer says : " Many a husband has buried
more wives than one, killed outright, ignorantly, yet effectually, by the brutality of this passion.
Reader, if thou knowest none such, thou knowest
not the cause of all the deaths that transpire
around thee ! And yet the pulpit, the press, the
lecture-room are silent in view of this vast, this
wicked waste of life."

There can be no exact rule laid down as to the
proper exercise of the generative function, as this
will depend on age, occupation, climate, season,
aliment, and numerous other influences.   However, sexual intercourse should never be indulged
in before the adult age, nor until there is a natural
desire.   It ought to be avoided whenever it produces more than temporary depression of spirits
or debility of the mental or physical state, also
during intoxication, excitement, mania, and when
there is venereal or any other disease of the sexual organs of either party.   It should be indulged
very moderately when under great mental or
bodily strain, or when the system is run down ;
and should be entirely abstained from during the
presence of the menses, and indulged in very

little, if at all, during pregnancy—the less the better. It is also injurious soon after a full meal, and when the mind is preoccupied. At the time of intercourse there must be no sense of discord, no repugnance ; it must depend on true, pure love, not insatiable sexual passion, and each should respond bodily and mentally to the nature of the other.

Intercourse should never be indulged in during the menstruating period. It is most injurious, contrary to all decency, and is never excusable. Nor should a woman at any time when she is averse to it be made to submit to intercourse to gratify the passion of her husband. Every woman has a right to her own person, and it is an outrage to try to deprive her of this right. Among the lower animals, the female always exercises the supremacy as to the conjugal relations ; and when she is in condition, and desires it, she informs the male in some way, and he, always ready, responds. For this purpose, females, whether fowls or quadrupeds, have peculiar cries and songs. The mewing of cats, lowing of cattle, cackling of fowls are familiar examples of solicitation of the male to reproduction. The supremacy of the female also exists among many of the heathen nations ; it is left for civilized man to descend lower than the savage or the animal in this respect. A man is always ready, or nearly so, to engage in intercourse ; but with a woman it is entirely different ; and on this account, and because she is the weaker of the two and is most concerned in the results, she should, as nature intended, always be the one to rule in this matter. This is woman's privilege, and nothing will retain her respect and love so much as to be allowed to exercise it ; and it seems an outrage that she should be denied this right, or *compelled* to bear a child when she does not wish it.

As to the Frequency of Intercourse.—This of course must depend on many circumstances, such as health, constitution, amount of exertion, and many others. Natural sexual enjoyment exalts and exhilarates vitality and improves the mental faculties and bodily functions ; but when too frequent, it enervates the body, induces sadness, disgust for life and even loss of reason. It soon exhausts the power of life, for intense life cannot be extensive. Experience teaches that the pleasures of love extinguish the fire of imagination, abate courage and genius and induce stupidity.

Dr. Ellis says :

"One party may be injured by a frequency which would not harm the other ; in such cases the duty of restraint is manifest, for in no instance has one a right to seriously injure the other for the sake of selfish gratification. But a suggestion to the young may not be amiss. Let no young man who is aware of having this propensity strong, ever marry a small-waisted, pale-faced, delicate woman, who is not accustomed to active labor or exercise, unless he has confidence that he can and is willing to restrain this passion to the extent that the welfare and health of his wife may require, even if it be total abstinence ; for an amount of indulgence which would be perfectly harmless to a strong, well-formed, robust, active woman may, with a small-waisted, delicate woman, whose bowels are pressed down upon the uterus and bladder, pressing them out of place, cause serious disease of the latter organs, and a train of symptoms which will make both husband and wife wretched, hurry the latter to a premature grave and leave the former with the painful consciousness that his sensuality has caused the death of her he has promised to love and protect. There is no gratification which draws so much upon the vitality of either man or woman as this, and the delicate man or woman has little to spare in this direction. Those of strong propensities and robust frames may well beware, then, how they unite with the delicate of the opposite sex, unless they are willing cheerfully to restrain their passions, and indulge rarely, if at all."

If half the women suffer disease and disorders from too frequent and improper intercourse, from the same cause—because their energy and life-force is sapped out—half the men fail in life, and cannot attain the highest of that to which their ability is capable.

The seminal fluid is a wonderful invigorator, and all physiologists agree that in the state of continence, to a certain extent, the whole organism is impressed with an extreme tension and vigor, exciting the brain and exalting the faculty of thought, besides giving courage, ability and strength. Men of great intellectual renown abstained from intercourse, or at least were extremely moderate. Newton, Kant, Fontanelle and Beethoven are such examples. Minerva, the goddess of genius, and all the muses were virgins.

People must judge for themselves as to the extent of intercourse, and it must depend entirely on circumstances ; but for their best interests, as an habitual thing, they should never exceed twice a week, and it would be best, under nearly every circumstance, if it were limited to once a week or even once a month. Especially should this be rigidly enforced before allowing a child to be generated ; and this leads up to the subject of generation.

Generation.

" That life is long which answers life's great end."
—YOUNG.

Every child has a right to be well born ; and parents should remember, when begetting a child, how much depends on what they are doing ; that not only the procreation of a rational being is concerned, but that its physical formation, constitution and cast of mind are at stake.

The art of raising fine stock has almost reached perfection ; why not that of having children ? Is it not far more important ? and yet the subject is ignored. No intelligent breeder would be willing to have his cattle bred under circumstances so unphysiological and harmful as he does his children. Parents are bound by honor and self-interest to have only well-born children ; in their offspring they have the opportunity to live over again—for great is the resemblance in body, mind, disease, virtue and vice. Yet sensible people every day are cursing their children with tainted blood, loathsome disease, madness, folly and unworthy dispositions.

If a child is to have a sound mind in a sound body it must come from sound seed. Parents must not allow generation to take place when they are in ill health or when the physical and mental powers are not at the best, either as a result of overwork, disease or dissipation. For this reason morning is generally the best time for reproduction, because the fatigues of the preceding day are dissipated by repose ; and at this time the majority of healthy individuals possess most virility.

It is well to say here that, as a general rule, it is best for people not to sleep together, whether adults or children, as one (or both) is liable to suffer ; and such sleep is seldom entirely refreshing.

If the system is worn out or overstrained, weak, imperfect children must result, or none at all. This is exemplified by the children of the great being few in number, and rarely possessed of any great degree of physique or intellect.

It is best not to allow conception to take place immediately after marriage, for the feasting and dissipation are most injurious to the child.

By protracted continence the species are improved and strengthened both in mind and body. Abstinence from sexual enjoyment for a few days or weeks, besides invigorating mind and body, greatly favors fecundation and the production of a healthy offspring.

Perfect organization of the offspring requires of the parents at the time of generation the most perfect harmony and enjoyment, and the most complete commingling of elements. They should be at one as much as possible, and almost lose, in the intensity of the sensation, the consciousness of individual, independent existence and surroundings.

Parents, do not stamp your offspring with an imperfect organization ; do not have children who will grow up to curse you for allowing them to inherit diseased bodies and vicious minds ; but bestow on them the greatest blessing, the richest fortune man can possess—good health. To do this, still more is required of the parents ; they must allow of only favorable influences to be brought to bear on the child in fœtal life ; and this brings us to the question :

Should Intercourse be Indulged in During Pregnancy?

" Take heed lest passion sway
Thy judgment to do aught which else free will
Would not admit."

—MILTON, *Paradise Lost.*

Every pregnant woman is the depository of a new and feeble being, at first imperceptible to the human eye, though it may be the future statesman, philosopher or ruler ; and which is powerfully though indirectly influenced by the moral, physical, and intellectual conditions of the mother. For the best interests of the offspring, then, it is not advisable, as a general rule, for the pregnant woman to indulge in or submit to sexual intercourse. This is nowhere better exemplified than in the lower animals, for nearly all mammiferous animals, with rare exceptions, refuse to admit the male after they are with young, because the great object of nature has been accomplished. The violation of this law by the human species often causes abortion, and seriously injures the health, to say nothing of the harm done to the child.

St. Augustine[1] says : " Conjugal modesty will not use pregnant or menstruating women."

Even among some of the heathen races in Asia and Africa, as well as among many tribes of Indians, it is held indecent to approach a pregnant woman.

Hippocrates thought that pregnant women who abstained had easier labors. **Galen** dwelt upon the liability to abortion from this cause at certain periods of pregnancy, the fruit being more easily detached when most tender and when approaching maturity.

Dr. Perrin says : " The fact that abstinence from physical love in pregnancy is the common rule of animals is certainly a strong argument in favor of urging similar abstinence on the part of men. Furthermore, practitioners are sometimes told by innocent husbands—more rarely by wives, who so often suffer in silence—that intercourse causes the latter great pain.

" Finally, this is a frequent cause of abortion ; at least one half of the cases of what is termed

---

[1] Third Book against Julian, c. 21.

spontaneous abortion are probably thus produced. Summing up the arguments in the affirmative of the question, it may be stated that indulgence in pregnancy is unnatural ; so far as woman is concerned it is generally odious, often painful, and in regard to the newly created being, frequently murderous.

" What can be alleged on the other side ? The peace of families and the chastity of husbands are secured by the indulgence. But suppose men were trained to believe that such indulgence is wrong, injurious to others and to themselves, would their amiability and chastity require to be purchased by a momentary pleasure ? Would they not rather learn to subdue and rule this otherwise imperious passion ? If Newton, Kant, Fontanelle and Beethoven could live their many honored years with no indulgence of passion, surely other men might abstain without injury. The ungoverned passion of man is prolific of evil ; and, like producing like, the father who has never learned self-control may give his son not only form and feature, but the germ of the same fierce, clamorous desire, which in its full development will prove a heritage of woe to that son and others. That which polite language veils under

the designation social evil, and which desolates
so many happy homes and brings its quick, black
harvest of misery, remorse, disease and death,
chiefly lives because man does not know aright,
does not duly reverence and honor woman and
keep in subjection that which may become one of
the monster passions in his heart, and is thus continued from generation to generation. Surely
prospective motherhood, woman, within whom
proceeds the evolution of the marvellous mys-
teries of creation, should be reverenced as worthy
of all thoughtful consideration, and ought to
have thrown around her all protective care. The
woman who has conceived is *enceinte*—that is,
ungirdled—in allusion to the ancient custom of
laying aside the girdle when pregnant and placing
it in the temple of the gods—at once a preparation
for the enlargement of the abdomen and a seeking
for Divine protection. Let her not fail of all human care while in this condition.

" Nature then offers unto man invitation and
opportunity to subordinate passion to reason, to
conscience, to will, to a higher love, and thus raise
himself above himself. A sensual age claims that
indulgence facilitates parturition and the most
sensual of husbands, finding their wives pregnant

very much against their wishes, will claim that they can now indulge freely and without fear, for matters can be no worse ! We do believe that intercourse in pregnancy has nothing to commend, nothing to excuse itself unto wise men ; and that virtuous abstinence on the part of the husband will be a blessing both to him and to his wife and to their posterity. It may be objected that the abstinence here advocated contradicts almost universal practice—a practice that frequently brings no evil. But how do we know it has no injurious results ? Admitting that the wife may, in the majority of cases, not patiently suffer, have no miscarriage, no pain, no nausea and vomiting increased or excited thereby, is there no violence done to the finer elements of a refined womanly nature ? Does such a women cheerfully accept it as the way of all, like Hiero's wife, who never perceived her husband's offensive breath, imagining that it was common to all men ? It seems that there might follow some lessening of mutual love, respect and reverence.

" So far as the husband is concerned, he learns no lesson of self-control, attains no self-mastery in this regard, and mars that ideal manhood which, in better hours and with nobler aspirations, he seeks to attain."

While it is undoubtedly injurious to mother and child that intercourse should be indulged in during pregnancy, in some cases it may be almost unavoidable. Should this be the case, then, it must be practised with the most extreme moderation—certainly not oftener than once in two or three weeks. Means should be adopted to control the passions, and this brings us to the discussion of this subject.

Measures for Controlling the Passions.

" He is most powerful who has himself in his power."
—SENECA.

The abnormal intensity of the passions is largely due to improper and too stimulating aliment, as ardent liquors of any kind, spiced meats, etc., because such improper diet causes irritation in the mucous membrane lining the digestive tract ; and as this is similar to that lining the genital organs, they also become irritated and congested. Another cause for this is the harboring and giving way to unchaste and wrong feelings. If a man engages in physical exercise, the muscles become developed ; if he engages in intellectual study, the brain becomes enlarged and developed ; and if his sexual organs are constantly in a state of excitement from allowing his attention to be continually directed to this sphere, then they must become abnormally developed.

The mind governs the sexual passion to a very large extent. To overcome sexual desire the attention must be diverted to some other object, for without this all effort is *useless*, as the more struggle that is made the more active becomes the centre in the brain which governs the sexual organs and so the more irritated the parts become. The moment the mind is centred on some other subject, the centre in the brain which governs sexual passion ceases to be active and so the irritation subsides. The mind must be diverted, then, to some other *object of interest.* "Nature abhors a vacuum ;" and if unchaste thoughts are to be crowded out, the mind must be filled with chaste ones or the evil ones will return.

The morbid amorous impulse is not to be wondered at, then, in those who are constantly goading the sexual passions into abnormal intensity by obscene associations, or by means of gross or

stimulating food and drink. To control and subdue the passions, not only is it necessary to keep
the attention away from sexual subjects, but to
avoid eating or drinking anything which may tend
to increase the amorous impulse—as, for instance,
spices, condiments, rich and highly seasoned food,
eggs and meats to any great extent, tea, alcoholic
liquors, tobacco, or any irritating or stimulating
food or drink. While alcoholic liquors stimulate
the passions, their excessive use is injurious to
generation and even produces impotency and sterility. Dissipated, weak men cannot beget strong
offspring, for the generating fluid must of neces-
sity be weak in such persons. When the spermatozoa or generating element in the male fluid are
weak and few in number, the sex of the child is
affected. This we will discuss in the following
chapter on the government of sex.

" That man lives twice that lives the first life well."
—HERRICK, *Hesperides Vertue.*

CHAPTER V.

Government of Sex.

" If you can look into the seeds of time,
  And say which grain will grow, and which will not,
  Speak . . . ."

—SHAKESPEARE.

SCIENCE has done a great deal to throw light on this subject ; and while it is not absolutely settled that the one sex or the other can be produced at will, it has been pretty well demonstrated that such is the case. Experiments have been made— almost entirely on animals, of course—and cases are on record where satisfactory results have also been obtained among the human race.

These experiments appear to verify the theory that at the time of conception the generative element which predominates, either in *amount* or *force*, decides the sex of the embryo. This theory has two applications, the one depending upon how long after menstruation conception takes place—that is, how far the egg has descended before becoming impregnated or fertilized ; the other application depends upon whichever parent is, at the time of conception, most energetic and vigorous.

M. Comaz, a Swiss agriculturist, succeeded twenty-nine times in twenty-nine cases in producing at will among his stock whichever sex he desired ; and others who have experimented have had equal or almost as great success. Many breeders of dogs, horses, cattle, sheep, etc., take advantage of this principle to secure whichever sex is most in demand.

This theory is also advocated by a professor of the Academy of Geneva, **M. Thury,** and widely experimented on in the breeding of stock. In practice, " conception in the first half of the time of viability, produces female offspring, and male in the latter half."

A physician who has observed the working of this theory writes : " Whenever intercourse has taken place in from two to six days after the cessation of the menses, girls have been produced ; and whenever intercourse has taken place in from nine to twelve days after the cessation of the menses, boys have been produced. In every case I ascertained not only the date at which the mother placed conception, but also the time when the menses ceased, the date of the first and subsequent intercourse for a month or more after the cessation of the menses."

It will be seen that in predetermining sex these authorities lay especial stress upon the date of conception as regards menstruation. The result may be modified, however, by the condition of strength and vitality of one or the other parent, the element of the stronger parent always tending to predominate.

To make this principle clear, it is necessary to explain that the ovum, or egg, comes from one of the ovaries—two small bodies situated on either side of the uterus—and in doing so it has to pass through the Fallopian tubes, which are connected with the uterus and are about four inches in length. To accomplish this it generally takes from eight to twelve days ; so that conception, as a rule, takes place within ten days or two weeks after menstruation. Now, if conception should take place soon after menstruation, the ovum is high up in the Fallopian tube ; as the spermatozoa have a long way to travel, only a few of them ever reach the egg, not in sufficient numbers to have a preponderation of the male element, so a female results. On the other hand, if conception takes place some time after menstruation, the egg is

necessarily low down in the tube, a large number
of the spermatozoa are able to reach it, and thus
it is likely that the male element will predominate. This may not be the case, though ; for if
the male is weak or not in a vigorous state, either
from ill-health, overwork, dissipation or too frequent intercourse, the spermatozoa would consequently have little power and be few in number,
so that even if the ovum were far advanced in the
tube, few might have vitality enough to reach and
impregnate it ; the result if any being a female.
But this, again, might vary a good deal ; for if
the female lacked vitality and vigor the result
might be the opposite, even if impregnation took
place soon after menstruation, when the egg was
high up in the tube. If both were weak the result
would probably be *nil*.

The above theory has been advocated by such
authorities as **Professor Brooks, Düring, Giru,
Haber, Hofacker, Knight, Kurg, Miles, Napier,
Ploss, Sadler, Geoffroy Saint-Hilaire.**

CHAPTER VI.

Sterility and Prevention of Infection.

'Something there was in her life incomplete, imperfect, unfinished."
—Longfellow.

There are many causes for sterility, some of which might be overcome and some that could never be remedied. In the first place, with two who are entirely neutral to each other, sterility must result. This is explained in treating of the temperaments.

If at the time of intercourse there should exist antipathy, disgust, hatred, extreme apathy or great fear, the result would likely be *nil*. Sterility often results from abuse of the marriage relation. People often abuse the function of generation by attempting to engender at all times, and too frequently ; and this in many cases is the cause of sterility ; for if the uterus is in an extreme and too frequent state of excitation, it may lose its power of retention ; and if men go to excesses,

the semen becomes thin and watery, the spermatozoa are few and weak or entirely absent, and so
sterility results.

It is necessary that the spermatozoa should be
retained in their receptacles for a few days to become prolific. For the most successful results, it
is always best to abstain from intercourse for a
couple of weeks—the longer the better, the more
quickly generation will take place and the better
will be the offspring.

Another cause of sterility is that the Fallopian
tubes leading into the uterus, as a result of inflammation, often from an infectious venereal disease,
become closed, so keeping the spermatozoa from
effecting an entrance.

Sometimes acrid discharges from the womb are
the cause of sterility, for any acid is destructive
to the spermatozoa ; and even if there is no visi-
ble discharge, it may be there in sufficient quantity to destroy the spermatozoa.

If the womb is in an unhealthy state from venereal disease or any other cause, while the ovum
may become impregnated and attach itself to the
womb and even go several months—perhaps to
the seventh—the fœtus is liable to become dis-
lodged, and thus miscarriage or abortion will take

place. If this is habitual, it is impossible to bear children.

Many of these troubles can only be remedied by medical treatment ; and we would advise those who suffer from them to place themselves under the care of their own physicians. The results in many cases will be satisfactory, for these cases are frequently curable.

Prevention of Infection.

Vaginal and uterine discharges, not necessarily specific, are often the means of causing trouble in the male organs ; but whether from this cause or any other, it is never necessary for this to happen if a thorough cleansing is rigidly enforced immediately after intercourse. The best mode, then, of preventing infection, no matter from what cause, is thorough and immediate ablution with water and soap ; or, if there is much risk, with a dilute solution of the disinfecting agents, such as permanganate of potash ; carbolic acid, strength of 1 to 60 ; corrosive sublimate, 1 to 5000 ; boracic acid, 1 to 50, etc., which can be obtained of any druggist. Such measures will prevent infection under almost any circumstances. Many authorities also recommend micturating immediately after intercourse.

CHAPTER VII.

Hygiene of Pregnancy.

" Health is the vital principle of bliss."

—Thomson.

The hygiene of pregnancy is a subject which is of much importance to every expectant mother, and yet it is one which is much neglected.

Gestation is a most important period to a woman, because under ordinary circumstances, if she takes proper care of herself and receives the same, her health will become greatly improved. Many weaknesses and ills will disappear, especially under proper care. We would advise every woman, when she becomes pregnant, to put herself under the care of her physician, and remain under his observation till after her child is born.

To the child *in utero,* gestation is the most important period of its life, because at this time it is just developing. The body and mind which are then being moulded will determine its future well-being, its success, its happiness and its usefulness.

To both mother and child, then, this is a most important period, and too much care for the welfare of both cannot be exercised.

In dealing with the hygiene of pregnancy, we will first take up the subject of bathing, then diet, regulation of the bowels, mode of dress, exercise and air, and sleep.

Bathing.

"Cleanliness is next to godliness" is a maxim especially true for the pregnant woman ; for it is not sufficient that a woman should be ordinarily clean during this critical period of her life. Her skin is now secreting more than ever the impurities from the body and daily baths are necessary, not only for cleanliness, for by going through a system of bathing the muscles become hardened and the system toned up. On rising in the morning, a cold sponge bath should be taken ; but if in a cold season of the year, the temperature of the water had better be regulated by the woman's health. It is better to begin with tepid water and decrease gradually. Later in the day—about three hours after breakfast—a sitz bath, which consists in bathing the hips only, should be taken.

If a regular sitz bath is not accessible, any round, flat vessel, large enough to allow one to sit down in, will answer the purpose. It should be filled with water to the depth of four or five inches. It is best to begin at a temperature of 90°, and gradually decrease till about 60° is reached. This bath especially needs to be taken cold, or at least cool, for much benefit to be derived from it. By carefully regulating the temperature of the bath and the room, there is no danger of taking cold or of any ill effects. In taking a sitz bath, it is only necessary to immerse the hips and not the limbs or any other part, so that the shoes and stockings, as well as much of the other clothes, may be kept on. After staying in the bath from three to ten minutes, dry off and follow with brisk friction with towel and hand for several moments. It is the reaction after any bath which gives it its value ; and no one should ever go into a bath feeling cold. This system of bathing makes the child a natural lover of cleanliness ; and more than this, to the mother's system it acts as a wonderful tonic. It helps to purify her system, and besides hardening her muscles, it invigorates her whole being. A short rest, and sleep if possible, are essential to the good results from this bath.

Diet.

This is of great importance to mother and child ; to the mother because it so largely assists in keeping her in good health ; to the child because it is necessary for it to have the proper kind of nourishment, and also because, through errors on the mother's part, it can be made a glutton. We mean by this latter that the mother should, for the sake of her child, be careful not to indulge her appetite too freely, and not to have her mind too much upon what goes into her stomach. Certain food is harmful at any time, but more especially at this time ; and the mother herself must be the judge of what is best. She will discard what she knows to be injurious to her, for what will agree with some will be harmful to others. However, she will be safe in not taking any kind of stimulants—even tea and coffee are injurious ; she should not take highly seasoned, rich or greasy food. Meat may agree with the mother perfectly under all ordinary circumstances, but if she wishes to avoid having a gross child she will take as little as possible during pregnancy. Fish and eggs to a limited extent make an excellent substitute. It is best always to eat a good breakfast, a moderate dinner and either a light evening meal or none at all ; and avoid strictly eating anything between meals. The digestion, though ordinarily strong, during this period is very easily upset ; and the greatest care will be necessary to avoid many troubles with the digestive organs.

There is a system of dieting which prevents the bones of the child's head becoming very hard, consequently the mother's sufferings are decreased during labor. Although such a diet might be thought injurious to the child, it appears not ; and experience seems to teach that if anything it is beneficial, as the child grows very rapidly after birth, soon making up for the lack of bony tissue when born. This system of diet consists in living on fruits and the grains growing in tropical climates—namely, rice, sago, tapioca, arrowroot and Indian corn ; the fruits consisting of all attainable fruits, especially oranges, lemons and apples. This seems a meagre diet, but many grateful mothers with hearty children can testify to its benefit. It is on the principle that the females of tropical climates have painless parturition, because their diet keeps the bones, especially the child's head, from becoming very hard.

This system is thoroughly dealt with by Dr.

Holbrook in his work, "Parturition without Pain," and in "Tokology," by Dr. A. B. Stockham.

Regulation of the Bowels.

Precautions will be taken to keep the bowels active. Among the best means for this purpose may be mentioned that of drinking a large glass of hot (not warm) water half an hour (not fifteen or twenty minutes) before meals. This washes out the stomach, and is beneficial to the bowels, liver and kidneys. Eating baked apples for breakfast is another excellent way to regulate the bowels. If, in spite of dieting and all precautions, the bowels are still inactive, which is not uncommon, the best thing then will be to make frequent use of injections of water into the bowels. As often as every other day will not be too much. This is not in the least harmful, and, on the contrary, will prove very beneficial, as well as giving relief and comfort. A quart of pleasantly warm water injected and allowed to remain as long as possible, while lying on the left side, will be found quite sufficient.

Mode of Dress During Pregnancy.

This is a matter which few think of any importance, but this is a great oversight. The dress should be loose and suspended from the shoulders. Corsets should not be worn. Many think that by wearing them during pregnancy, they help the figure to return to its natural shape after childbirth, but this is an error.

The feet should be warm and dry, and commonsense shoes should be worn.

Exercise and Fresh Air.

The mother should be in the open air as much as possible. She should take as much regular exercise as she can without exhaustion. We mean by this walking at least two or three miles a day, beginning gradually, and indulging in any exercise that is *enjoyable*. Many have an idea that because a new life is going on within them they must " eat for two." This is a fallacy, for the growth is so gradual and so slight that this care is quite unnecessary. But it *is* necessary to breathe for two. This is most essential, and deep breathing should be practised at least half a dozen times a day. This consists in taking as deep a breath as possible and retaining it for a moment ; then expel slowly. It must be done in the erect position, with chest thrown forward, and with energy. Of course the air must be pure, outdoor air.

Sleep.

A pregnant woman needs good, sound, refreshing sleep, in a cool, well-ventilated room ; and she will do much better if she sleeps alone. Every woman would be better of a short sleep during the day, preferably the morning ; and the pregnant woman especially needs this. It should always be taken after the sitz bath and before dinner.

In the present age of enlightenment the danger in childbirth is very small, and the suffering has likewise been greatly decreased, owing to the light thrown on the hygienic mode of living during pregnancy and the use of means to alleviate any great pain at childbirth.

Nothing improves the health of most women so much as bearing children. It increases the vitality, improves the complexion. Many a weak, delicate woman has bloomed into a healthy, robust mother.

According to her capability, and as to how much she is deserving of the name of a true woman, will an expectant mother follow out the simple rules herein contained.

> " Time is indeed a precious boon,
>   But with the boon a task is given ;
>   The heart must learn its duty well
>   To man on earth and God in heaven."
>   —ELIZA COOK.

CONCLUSION.

"All persons possessing any portion of power ought to be strongly and awfully impressed with an idea that they act in trust, and that they are to account for their conduct in that trust to the one great Master, Author and Founder of society."—BURKE.

LET no man or woman lay these thoughts aside and say, "I am not a parent ; this is not for me." The idea is erroneous that the diseases and crimes of others are no concern of ours ; for all disease, all uncleanness, all infection that exists in one place is liable to affect others. No place is exempt from this invasion, for disease can be conveyed with the greatest readiness by insects, such as flies ; a current of air can carry infection for miles, and so with persons, mail matter, etc. Who knows what home may next be invaded or what beloved one may next be taken !

Therefore it behooves every one to do all in his power to limit the amount of disease existing at present, and if possible diminish it in future generations. This can only be done by knowing how to have healthy children or none at all, and by knowing how to care for the ones we do have. On this account, even if the reader is not an intending parent, it is certainly to his interest to direct the attention of his parent friends to this matter, that his own surroundings may be made more comfortable and secure.

It is the same with crime. Is not every man paying to the State his portion for the support of imprisoned criminals? Are not hundreds of innocent human beings deprived every year of their property, their health, and even their lives because of the unrestrained criminals which abound in every land? That his own life and his own property may be secure, it is to every man's interest to aid in reducing the number of these criminals, and this can only be done by knowing how to have well-born children or none at all.

If one quarter the time, talent, and money which the civilized world now spends on courts, jails, penitentiaries, asylums, poor-houses, hospitals and reform schools were applied to producing only well-born children, and to educate and train these, then all the former would soon be little needed. Men would be ready to arbitrate rather than dispute, to reason rather than quarrel, rob or murder ; and, furthermore, they would have the strength of character sufficient to resist baneful habits, and would be of such sound physique that they would not easily succumb to disease.

That this can be accomplished is beyond doubt, but it must be done not only through the influence and support of those who have ability, power and means, but through the individual effort, whether much or little, of every capable man and woman. If the weak, the imperfect, the vicious or the diseased had been able to prevent their condition, they would have done so ; and so it is not from them, but from other sources that reformation must come. Besides individual effort, it is the duty of governments and municipalities to act on this question, for there must be legislation to *prevent* crime, disease and inability, and not to battle unsuccessfully with its suppression ; and it is only by such effort of individual and State that a healthier, wiser, happier, nobler generation will result.

AUTHOR'S NOTE.

THE subjects of this book are of such interest and importance to all, especially the subject of pre natal influence, that I would earnestly request that those who can furnish undoubted cases of pre-natal influence will do so. Cases affecting the mental or moral character are especially desired. If such cases have resulted favorably, then others will profit by knowing of them ; if they have been unfavorable, then they will be able to take advantage of the experience of others and so guard against what will result harmfully. The names connected with the case, if so desired, will be withheld, except that of the medical authority. I would also request that all the details be given as clearly and concisely as possible. Especially regarding the nature of the impression, the results in the child and the time or times of pregnancy at which it occurred. I would repeat that the cases must come from undoubted sources ; the writer should be able to vouch for the details.

901 *Third Avenue, Louisville, Ky.*

INDEX.

BOOKS

From the Press of the Arena Publishing Company.

Jason Edwards: An Average Man.

By HAMLIN GARLAND.   A powerful and realistic story of to-day.   Price: paper, 50 cents; cloth, $1.00.

Who Lies?   An Interrogation.

By BLUM and ALEXANDER.   A book that is well worth reading.   Price: paper, 50 cents; cloth, $1.00.

Main Travelled Roads.

Six Mississippi Valley stories.   By HAMLIN GARLAND.

"The sturdy spirit of true democracy runs through this book."— *Review of Reviews.*

Price: paper, 50 cents; cloth, $1.00.

Irrepressible Conflict Between Two World-Theories.

By Rev. MINOT J. SAVAGE.   The most powerful presentation of Theistic Evolution *versus* Orthodoxy that has ever appeared.   Price: paper, 50 cents; cloth, $1.00.

For sale by all booksellers.   Sent postpaid upon receipt of the price.

Arena Publishing Company,

Copley Square,   BOSTON, MASS.

From the Press of the Arena Publishing Company.

Songs.

By NEITH BOYCE. Illustrated with original drawings by ETHELWYN WELLS CONREY. A beautiful gift book. Bound in white and gold. Price, postpaid, $1.25.

The Finished Creation, and Other Poems.

By BENJAMIN HATHAWAY, author of "The League of the Iroquois," "Art Life," and other Poems. Handsomely bound in white parchment vellum, stamped in silver. Price, postpaid, $1.25.

Wit and Humor of the Bible.

By Rev. MARION D. SHUTTER, D.D. A brilliant and reverent treatise. Published only in cloth. Price, postpaid, $1.50.

Son of Man; or, Sequel to Evolution.

By CELESTIA ROOT LANG. Published only in cloth.

This work, in many respects, very remarkably discusses the next step in the Evolution of Man. It is in perfect touch with advanced Christian Evolutionary thought, but takes a step beyond the present position of Religion Leaders.

Price, postpaid, $1.25.

For sale by all booksellers. Sent postpaid upon receipt of the price.

Arena Publishing Company,

Copley Square,   BOSTON, MASS.

From the Press of the Arena Publishing Company.

The Rise of the Swiss Republic.

By W. D. MCCRACKAN, A. M.

It contains over four hundred pages, printed from new and handsome type, on a fine quality of heavy paper. The margins are wide, and the volume is richly bound in cloth.

Price, postpaid, $3.00.

Sultan to Sultan.

By M. FRENCH-SHELDON (Bebe Bwana).

Being a thrilling account of a remarkable expedition to the Masai and other hostile tribes of East Africa, which was planned and commanded by this intrepid woman. **A Sumptuous Volume of Travels.** Handsomely illustrated; printed on coated paper and richly bound in African red silk-finished cloth.

Price, postpaid, $5.00.

The League of the Iroquois.

By BENJAMIN HATHAWAY.

It is instinct with good taste and poetic feeling, affluent of pictur-esque description and graceful portraiture, and its versification is fairly melodious. — *Harper's Magazine.*

Has the charm of Longfellow's "Hiawatha." — *Albany Evening Journal.*

Of rare excellence and beauty. — *American Wesleyan.*

Evinces fine qualities of imagination, and is distinguished by re-markable grace and fluency. — *Boston Gazette.*

The publication of this poem alone may well serve as a mile-post in marking the pathway of American literature. The work is a marvel of legendary lore, and will be appreciated by every earnest reader. — *Boston Times.*

Price, postpaid, cloth, $1.00 ; Red Line edition, $1.50.

For sale by all booksellers. Sent postpaid upon receipt of the price.

Arena Publishing Company,

Copley Square,   **BOSTON, MASS.**

ZENIA THE VESTAL.

By MARGARET B. PEEKE, author of "Born of Flame," etc. Assisted by the Brotherhood and by order of the Hierophant Egyptian and Alcantras of Grenada, under direction of the Algerine. This is a book embodying the occult laws of spiritual development, as given by the wise men of other lands, some of which laws are now presented in English for the first time. The vehicle of these teachings is a story, scenes of which are laid in Europe, but the characters are American. Titles of some of the chapters: Fate, Alps, Destiny, Reunion, Hermitage, Vibrations, Paris, Interlude, Egypt, Flight, Prophecy, Chamouni, Insights, Madeira, Farewell, St. Cloud, Anticipation. *Price, in handsome cloth,* $2.

IT IS POSSIBLE.

By HELEN VAN-ANDERSON. The author shows wonderful insight into child-life, and the story is delightful. *Price: post-paid, paper,* 50 *cents; cloth,* $1.25.

"It Is Possible," by Mrs. Helen Van-Anderson, is a story written evidently by a thinker of more than usual ability. — *Inter-Ocean, Chicago.*

"It is Possible," by Mrs. Helen Van-Anderson, is a work deserving of a large sale and of being widely read. No one can read the book without partaking, in some measure at least, of the intense spirituality which pervades the story. — *American Farm News.*

THE RIGHT KNOCK.

By HELEN VAN-ANDERSON. 318 pages in handsome cloth. *Price, post-paid,* $1.25.

If a book comes from the heart, it will contrive to reach the heart. — *Carlyle.*

"The Right Knock" is presented with no other apology than this, it has come from the heart. — *Author's Preface.*

For sale by all booksellers.   *Sent post-paid upon receipt of the price.*

Arena Publishing Company,

Copley Square,   Boston, Mass.

.˙. *From the Press of the Arena Publishing Company.* .˙.

CIVILIZATION'S INFERNO.

STUDIES IN THE SOCIAL CELLAR.

BY B. O. FLOWER.

A bold, unconventional book which in a merciless manner lays bare the criminal extravagance, the disgusting flunkyism, and the immorality found in what the author terms the "Froth of Society."

It fearlessly contrasts the criminal extravagance and moral effeminacy of the slothful rich with the terrible social, moral, and physical condition of the ignorant, starving, and degraded poor.

It carries the reader into the social cellar where uninvited poverty abounds, and from there into the sub-cellar, or the world of the criminal poor.

It is rich in suggestive hints, and should be in the hands of every thoughtful man and woman in America.

TABLE OF CONTENTS.—I. Introductory Chapter. II. Society's Exiles. III. Two Hours in the Social Cellar. IV. The Democracy of Darkness. V. Why the Ishmaelites Multiply. VI. The Froth and the Dregs. VII. A Pilgrimage and a Vision. VIII. What of the Morrow.

Price: paper, 50 *cents; cloth*, $1.25.

PRESS COMMENTS.

It is a strong appeal to the Christian civilization of the times to arise and change the current of human misery which in these modern times is driving with such resistless force. —*Chicago Daily Inter-Ocean.*

A thoughtful work by a thoughtful man, and should turn the minds of many who are now ignorant or careless to the condition of the countless thousands who live in the "social cellar." — *Courier-Journal, Louisville, Ky.*

Society, as it is now constituted, is nothing less than a sleeping volcano. Who dares to say how soon the upheaval will come, or whether it can be evaded by the adoption of prompt measures of relief? Certainly the condition of the lower social strata calls for immediate action on the part of those whose safety is at stake. Mr. Flower has accomplished a great work, in setting forth the exact truth of the matter, without any effort at palliation. —*Boston Beacon.*

For sale by all booksellers.   *Sent post-paid upon receipt of the price.*

Arena Publishing Company,

Copley Square,   Boston, Mass.

BOOKS

BOOKS

∴ From the press of the Arena Publishing Company. ∴

AI; A SOCIAL VISION

By Rev. Charles S. Daniel.

For To=day.

www.ingramcontent.com/pod-product-compliance
Lightning Source LLC
Chambersburg PA
CBHW030618030726

47497CB00006B/1552